85 Barbecue and Grilling Recipes for Home

By: Kelly Johnson

Table of Contents

Recipes

- Smoky Maple Glazed BBQ Chicken Skewers
- Grilled Lemon Garlic Shrimp Skewers
- Bourbon Brown Sugar BBQ Ribs
- Grilled Vegetable and Halloumi Skewers
- Teriyaki Pineapple Chicken Skewers
- Mediterranean Grilled Lamb Chops
- Chimichurri Grilled Steak
- Grilled Vegetable Quesadillas
- Grilled Salmon with Lemon-Dill Sauce
- Grilled Portobello Mushroom Burgers
- Grilled Honey-Lime Chicken Skewers
- Grilled Shrimp Tacos with Avocado Lime Crema
- Grilled Veggie and Halloumi Quinoa Bowl
- Grilled Teriyaki Pineapple Salmon
- Grilled Vegetable Stuffed Portobello Mushrooms
- Grilled Lemon-Herb Chicken Drumsticks
- Grilled Garlic-Lime Shrimp Tacos
- Grilled Teriyaki Veggie Skewers
- Grilled Peach and Burrata Salad
- Grilled Veggie and Pesto Flatbread
- Grilled Chicken Caesar Salad Wraps
- Grilled Pineapple Chicken Skewers
- Grilled Eggplant and Mozzarella Stacks

- Grilled Teriyaki Salmon Bowls
- Grilled Halloumi and Vegetable Skewers
- Grilled Chimichurri Steak Tacos
- Grilled Vegetable and Quinoa Stuffed Bell Peppers
- Grilled Honey-Lime Chicken Skewers
- Grilled Portobello Mushroom Burgers
- Grilled Veggie Quesadillas with Cilantro Lime Crema
- Grilled Lemon-Garlic Shrimp Skewers
- Grilled Teriyaki Pineapple Chicken Skewers
- Grilled Caprese Stuffed Portobello Mushrooms
- Grilled Lemon Herb Salmon
- Grilled Vegetable and Pesto Pasta Salad
- Grilled Teriyaki Tofu Skewers
- Grilled Southwest Chicken Salad
- Grilled Peach and Halloumi Salad
- Grilled Cilantro-Lime Chicken Tacos
- Grilled Teriyaki Pineapple Shrimp Skewers
- Grilled Vegetable and Hummus Wrap
- Grilled Salmon with Lemon-Dill Butter
- Grilled Vegetable Quinoa Bowl with Avocado-Lime Dressing
- Grilled Chimichurri Flank Steak
- Grilled Mediterranean Veggie and Halloumi Skewers
- Grilled Honey Mustard Glazed Chicken Thighs
- Grilled Teriyaki Veggie and Tofu Skewers
- Grilled Lemon Garlic Shrimp Skewers
- Grilled Caprese Portobello Mushrooms
- Grilled Veggie and Hummus Wrap

- Grilled Pineapple Chicken Skewers with Teriyaki Glaze
- Grilled Veggie Quesadillas with Avocado Salsa
- Grilled Lemon Herb Salmon
- Grilled Peach and Goat Cheese Salad
- Grilled Garlic-Lime Chicken Skewers
- Grilled Portobello Mushroom Burgers with Basil Aioli
- Grilled Teriyaki Pineapple Turkey Burgers
- Grilled Teriyaki Salmon Bowls
- Grilled Herb-Marinated Lamb Chops
- Grilled Sweet Potato and Black Bean Quesadillas
- Grilled Mediterranean Chicken Salad
- Grilled Shrimp Tacos with Avocado Lime Crema
- Grilled Vegetable and Halloumi Skewers with Lemon Herb Marinade
- Grilled Lemon Garlic Shrimp Pasta
- Grilled Honey Mustard Chicken Skewers
- Grilled Veggie and Hummus Wraps
- Grilled Pineapple Chicken Skewers with Teriyaki Glaze
- Grilled Tofu and Vegetable Kebabs with Peanut Sauce
- Grilled Eggplant and Mozzarella Panini
- Grilled Lemon Herb Salmon with Asparagus
- Grilled Portobello Mushroom Burgers with Balsamic Glaze
- Grilled Vegetable and Quinoa Stuffed Peppers
- Grilled Teriyaki Tofu Skewers with Pineapple
- Grilled Caprese Stuffed Portobello Mushrooms
- Grilled Lemon Herb Chicken with Mediterranean Couscous Salad
- Grilled Vegetable Quesadillas with Avocado Lime Dip
- Grilled Shrimp Tacos with Mango Salsa

- Grilled Chicken Caesar Salad Wraps
- Grilled Vegetable and Pesto Pizza
- Grilled Teriyaki Salmon with Pineapple Salsa
- Grilled Vegetable and Quinoa Stuffed Acorn Squash
- Grilled Honey Mustard Chicken Skewers
- Grilled Halloumi and Vegetable Kabobs
- Grilled Portobello Mushroom Steaks with Chimichurri Sauce
- Grilled Vegetable and Goat Cheese Stuffed Bell Peppers
- Lemon Blueberry Cheesecake Cookies
- Chocolate Hazelnut Thumbprint Cookies
- Oatmeal Raisin Cookies with Pecans
- Triple Chocolate Chip Cookies
- Peanut Butter and Jelly Thumbprint Cookies
- Snickerdoodle Cookies

Smoky Maple Glazed BBQ Chicken Skewers

Ingredients:

- 2 lbs boneless, skinless chicken thighs, cut into 1-inch cubes
- Wooden skewers, soaked in water for 30 minutes
- 1/2 cup maple syrup
- 1/4 cup soy sauce
- 2 tablespoons olive oil
- 2 cloves garlic, minced
- 1 teaspoon smoked paprika
- 1 teaspoon ground cumin
- 1/2 teaspoon cayenne pepper (adjust to taste)
- Salt and black pepper to taste
- Fresh cilantro, chopped (for garnish)

Instructions:

In a bowl, whisk together maple syrup, soy sauce, olive oil, minced garlic, smoked paprika, ground cumin, cayenne pepper, salt, and black pepper to create the marinade.
Place the chicken cubes in a resealable plastic bag or a shallow dish. Pour half of the marinade over the chicken, making sure each piece is coated. Reserve the remaining marinade for basting.
Seal the bag or cover the dish and refrigerate for at least 2 hours, or ideally overnight, to let the flavors infuse into the chicken.
Preheat the grill to medium-high heat.
Thread the marinated chicken cubes onto the soaked wooden skewers, ensuring an even distribution.
Place the skewers on the preheated grill and cook for 10-15 minutes, turning occasionally, until the chicken is cooked through and has a nice char.
During the last few minutes of grilling, brush the reserved marinade over the skewers, creating a flavorful glaze. Be sure to turn the skewers to coat all sides evenly.
Once the chicken is cooked and has a delicious caramelized glaze, remove the skewers from the grill.
Sprinkle chopped fresh cilantro over the skewers for a burst of freshness.
Serve the Smoky Maple Glazed BBQ Chicken Skewers hot, accompanied by your favorite barbecue sides and sauces.

Enjoy the irresistible combination of smoky flavors, sweet maple glaze, and perfectly grilled chicken with this crowd-pleasing barbecue recipe!

Grilled Lemon Garlic Shrimp Skewers

Ingredients:

- 1 lb large shrimp, peeled and deveined
- Wooden skewers, soaked in water for 30 minutes
- 3 tablespoons olive oil
- 3 cloves garlic, minced
- Zest of 1 lemon
- Juice of 1 lemon
- 1 teaspoon dried oregano
- 1 teaspoon smoked paprika
- Salt and black pepper to taste
- Fresh parsley, chopped (for garnish)

Instructions:

In a bowl, combine olive oil, minced garlic, lemon zest, lemon juice, dried oregano, smoked paprika, salt, and black pepper to create the marinade.

Add the peeled and deveined shrimp to the marinade, ensuring that each shrimp is well-coated. Allow the shrimp to marinate for at least 20-30 minutes.

Preheat the grill to medium-high heat.

Thread the marinated shrimp onto the soaked wooden skewers.

Place the shrimp skewers on the preheated grill and cook for 2-3 minutes per side or until the shrimp turn pink and opaque. Be cautious not to overcook to keep them tender.

During the last minute of grilling, brush some additional marinade over the shrimp for extra flavor.

Remove the shrimp skewers from the grill and transfer them to a serving platter.

Sprinkle freshly chopped parsley over the grilled shrimp for a burst of color and freshness.

Serve the Grilled Lemon Garlic Shrimp Skewers hot, either as an appetizer or as a main course with a side of rice or a light salad.

Enjoy the succulent combination of zesty lemon, aromatic garlic, and perfectly grilled shrimp in this easy and flavorful recipe!

Bourbon Brown Sugar BBQ Ribs

Ingredients:

- 2 racks of baby back ribs
- Salt and black pepper to taste
- 1 cup bourbon
- 1 cup brown sugar
- 1/2 cup ketchup
- 1/4 cup apple cider vinegar
- 1/4 cup soy sauce
- 2 tablespoons Dijon mustard
- 1 tablespoon Worcestershire sauce
- 1 teaspoon smoked paprika
- 1 teaspoon garlic powder
- 1 teaspoon onion powder
- 1/2 teaspoon cayenne pepper (adjust to taste)

Instructions:

Preheat your grill to medium-low heat, setting it up for indirect grilling.

Remove the membrane from the back of the ribs and season both sides with salt and black pepper.

In a saucepan over medium heat, combine bourbon, brown sugar, ketchup, apple cider vinegar, soy sauce, Dijon mustard, Worcestershire sauce, smoked paprika, garlic powder, onion powder, and cayenne pepper. Bring the mixture to a simmer and cook for about 15 minutes, stirring occasionally, until it thickens into a rich barbecue sauce.

Reserve half of the barbecue sauce for basting during grilling.

Place the seasoned ribs on the indirect heat side of the grill, bone side down. Close the lid and let them cook for about 1.5 to 2 hours, or until the meat starts to pull away from the bones.

Brush the ribs generously with the reserved barbecue sauce during the last 30 minutes of grilling, turning occasionally to ensure even coating.

Continue grilling until the ribs are tender and have a beautiful caramelized crust.

Carefully remove the ribs from the grill and let them rest for a few minutes.

Slice the ribs between the bones and arrange them on a serving platter.

Serve the Bourbon Brown Sugar BBQ Ribs with extra barbecue sauce on the side, and enjoy the perfect balance of smoky, sweet, and savory flavors.

These bourbon-infused ribs are sure to be a hit at your next barbecue gathering!

Grilled Vegetable and Halloumi Skewers

Ingredients:

- 1 block (about 8 oz) halloumi cheese, cut into cubes
- 1 zucchini, sliced into rounds
- 1 red bell pepper, cut into chunks
- 1 yellow bell pepper, cut into chunks
- 1 red onion, cut into wedges
- Cherry tomatoes
- Wooden skewers, soaked in water for 30 minutes
- 3 tablespoons olive oil
- 2 tablespoons balsamic vinegar
- 2 cloves garlic, minced
- 1 teaspoon dried oregano
- Salt and black pepper to taste
- Fresh basil leaves (for garnish)

Instructions:

Preheat the grill to medium-high heat.

In a bowl, whisk together olive oil, balsamic vinegar, minced garlic, dried oregano, salt, and black pepper to create the marinade.

Thread the halloumi cubes and assorted vegetables onto the soaked wooden skewers, alternating for a colorful mix.

Brush the skewers with the prepared marinade, ensuring even coating on all sides.

Place the skewers on the preheated grill and cook for about 8-10 minutes, turning occasionally, until the vegetables are tender and the halloumi has a golden brown crust.

During grilling, you can brush the skewers with additional marinade for extra flavor.

Once the skewers are done, transfer them to a serving platter.

Garnish with fresh basil leaves for a burst of aromatic freshness.

Serve the Grilled Vegetable and Halloumi Skewers hot, either as a flavorful appetizer or as a delightful side dish.

Enjoy the vibrant combination of grilled vegetables and savory halloumi cheese with this easy and healthy recipe!

Teriyaki Pineapple Chicken Skewers

Ingredients:

- 2 lbs boneless, skinless chicken thighs, cut into 1-inch cubes
- Wooden skewers, soaked in water for 30 minutes
- 1 cup pineapple juice
- 1/2 cup soy sauce
- 1/4 cup honey
- 2 tablespoons rice vinegar
- 2 cloves garlic, minced
- 1 teaspoon ginger, grated
- 1 tablespoon cornstarch (optional, for thickening)
- Pineapple chunks, for skewering
- Green onions, chopped (for garnish)
- Sesame seeds (for garnish)

Instructions:

In a bowl, whisk together pineapple juice, soy sauce, honey, rice vinegar, minced garlic, and grated ginger to create the teriyaki marinade.

Reserve a small portion of the marinade for basting during grilling.

Place the chicken cubes in a resealable plastic bag or a shallow dish. Pour the majority of the teriyaki marinade over the chicken, making sure each piece is coated. Marinate in the refrigerator for at least 1 hour, or ideally overnight.

Preheat the grill to medium-high heat.

Thread the marinated chicken cubes and pineapple chunks onto the soaked wooden skewers, alternating for a delicious combination.

Grill the skewers for about 10-12 minutes, turning occasionally, until the chicken is fully cooked and has a caramelized glaze.

While grilling, baste the skewers with the reserved teriyaki marinade for extra flavor.

If desired, you can thicken the remaining marinade with cornstarch on the stovetop to create a glaze for drizzling over the skewers.

Transfer the skewers to a serving platter.

Garnish with chopped green onions and sprinkle sesame seeds over the top.

Serve the Teriyaki Pineapple Chicken Skewers hot, accompanied by rice or your favorite side dishes. Enjoy the perfect balance of sweet and savory flavors with a hint of tropical pineapple!

Mediterranean Grilled Lamb Chops

Ingredients:

- 8 lamb chops, trimmed of excess fat
- 1/4 cup olive oil
- 3 tablespoons red wine vinegar
- 3 cloves garlic, minced
- 1 tablespoon dried oregano
- 1 teaspoon dried thyme
- 1 teaspoon ground cumin
- Salt and black pepper to taste
- Lemon wedges (for serving)
- Fresh mint leaves (for garnish)

Instructions:

In a bowl, whisk together olive oil, red wine vinegar, minced garlic, dried oregano, dried thyme, ground cumin, salt, and black pepper to create the marinade.

Place the lamb chops in a shallow dish and pour the marinade over them. Ensure each chop is well-coated. Marinate in the refrigerator for at least 2 hours, allowing the flavors to infuse.

Preheat the grill to medium-high heat.

Remove the lamb chops from the marinade and let excess marinade drip off.

Grill the lamb chops for about 3-4 minutes per side for medium-rare, or adjust the cooking time to your desired level of doneness.

During grilling, you can brush the chops with any remaining marinade for extra flavor.

Once the lamb chops are cooked to your liking, transfer them to a serving platter.

Squeeze fresh lemon wedges over the lamb chops just before serving.

Garnish with fresh mint leaves for a burst of herbal freshness.

Serve the Mediterranean Grilled Lamb Chops hot, accompanied by your favorite Mediterranean sides such as couscous, Greek salad, or roasted vegetables.

Enjoy the robust and flavorful taste of these perfectly grilled Mediterranean lamb chops!

Chimichurri Grilled Steak

Ingredients:

For the Steak:

- 4 boneless ribeye or sirloin steaks (about 1 inch thick)
- Salt and black pepper to taste
- 2 tablespoons olive oil

For the Chimichurri Sauce:

- 1 cup fresh parsley, finely chopped
- 1/4 cup fresh cilantro, finely chopped
- 3 cloves garlic, minced
- 1/2 cup extra virgin olive oil
- 3 tablespoons red wine vinegar
- 1 teaspoon dried oregano
- 1/2 teaspoon red pepper flakes (adjust to taste)
- Salt and black pepper to taste
- Juice of 1 lime

Instructions:

Preheat the grill to high heat.

Season the steaks with salt and black pepper on both sides. Drizzle olive oil over the steaks and rub to coat them evenly.

In a bowl, combine chopped parsley, chopped cilantro, minced garlic, extra virgin olive oil, red wine vinegar, dried oregano, red pepper flakes, salt, black pepper, and lime juice to create the chimichurri sauce. Mix well and set aside.

Place the seasoned steaks on the preheated grill and cook for about 4-5 minutes per side for medium-rare, or adjust the cooking time to your preferred doneness.

During grilling, you can baste the steaks with any remaining chimichurri sauce for added flavor.

Once the steaks are cooked to your liking, transfer them to a cutting board and let them rest for a few minutes.

Slice the steaks against the grain into strips.

Drizzle additional chimichurri sauce over the sliced steak and serve the remaining sauce on the side.

Garnish with additional fresh herbs for a vibrant presentation.

Serve the Chimichurri Grilled Steak hot, accompanied by roasted vegetables, mashed potatoes, or your favorite side dishes.

Enjoy the bold and zesty flavors of chimichurri complementing perfectly grilled steaks!

Grilled Vegetable Quesadillas

Ingredients:

For the Marinade:

- 1/4 cup olive oil
- 2 tablespoons balsamic vinegar
- 2 cloves garlic, minced
- 1 teaspoon dried oregano
- Salt and black pepper to taste

For the Quesadillas:

- 4 large flour tortillas
- 1 zucchini, sliced
- 1 red bell pepper, thinly sliced
- 1 yellow bell pepper, thinly sliced
- 1 red onion, thinly sliced
- 1 cup cherry tomatoes, halved
- 1 cup shredded Monterey Jack cheese
- 1 cup shredded cheddar cheese
- Fresh cilantro, chopped (for garnish)
- Sour cream and salsa (for serving)

Instructions:

Preheat the grill to medium-high heat.

In a bowl, whisk together olive oil, balsamic vinegar, minced garlic, dried oregano, salt, and black pepper to create the marinade.

Place the sliced zucchini, red bell pepper, yellow bell pepper, red onion, and cherry tomatoes in a large bowl. Pour the marinade over the vegetables and toss to coat evenly. Let them marinate for about 15-20 minutes.

Thread the marinated vegetables onto skewers or use a grill basket for easy grilling.

Grill the vegetables for about 5-7 minutes, turning occasionally, until they are tender and have a nice char.

Remove the vegetables from the grill and set aside.

Place a large tortilla on a flat surface. Sprinkle a layer of shredded Monterey Jack and cheddar cheese over half of the tortilla.

Add a portion of the grilled vegetables on top of the cheese.

Fold the tortilla over to cover the filling, creating a half-moon shape.

Repeat the process for the remaining tortillas.

Place the filled tortillas on the grill and cook for about 2-3 minutes per side, or until the cheese is melted and the tortillas have grill marks.

Remove the quesadillas from the grill and let them cool for a minute before slicing.

Garnish with chopped fresh cilantro.

Serve the Grilled Vegetable Quesadillas hot, accompanied by sour cream and salsa on the side.

Enjoy these delicious and colorful grilled vegetable quesadillas as a tasty and satisfying meal!

Grilled Salmon with Lemon-Dill Sauce

Ingredients:

For the Salmon:

- 4 salmon fillets (about 6 ounces each)
- Salt and black pepper to taste
- 2 tablespoons olive oil
- 1 teaspoon smoked paprika
- 1 teaspoon garlic powder
- Lemon wedges (for serving)

For the Lemon-Dill Sauce:

- 1/2 cup plain Greek yogurt
- 2 tablespoons mayonnaise
- Zest of 1 lemon
- 2 tablespoons fresh lemon juice
- 2 tablespoons fresh dill, chopped
- 1 tablespoon capers, chopped
- Salt and black pepper to taste

Instructions:

Preheat the grill to medium-high heat.

Season the salmon fillets with salt, black pepper, smoked paprika, and garlic powder.

Drizzle olive oil over the fillets and rub to coat evenly.

In a small bowl, combine Greek yogurt, mayonnaise, lemon zest, lemon juice, chopped fresh dill, chopped capers, salt, and black pepper to create the lemon-dill sauce. Mix well and refrigerate until ready to serve.

Place the seasoned salmon fillets on the preheated grill, skin side down. Grill for about 4-5 minutes per side, or until the salmon is cooked through and has a nice grill marks. During grilling, you can baste the salmon with a little extra olive oil or lemon juice if desired.

Remove the salmon from the grill and transfer to a serving platter.

Serve the Grilled Salmon with Lemon-Dill Sauce, drizzling the sauce over the top of each fillet.

Garnish with additional fresh dill and serve with lemon wedges on the side.

Pair the grilled salmon with your favorite side dishes, such as roasted vegetables or a quinoa salad.

Enjoy this light and flavorful grilled salmon dish with the zesty kick of lemon-dill sauce!

Grilled Portobello Mushroom Burgers

Ingredients:

For the Marinade:

- 1/4 cup balsamic vinegar
- 2 tablespoons soy sauce
- 2 tablespoons olive oil
- 2 cloves garlic, minced
- 1 teaspoon dried thyme
- Salt and black pepper to taste

For the Mushroom Burgers:

- 4 large portobello mushroom caps, cleaned and stems removed
- 4 whole-grain burger buns
- 1 cup arugula or baby spinach
- 1 large tomato, sliced
- Red onion, thinly sliced
- 4 slices Swiss or provolone cheese (optional)
- Dijon mustard and mayonnaise (for spreading)

Instructions:

Preheat the grill to medium-high heat.

In a bowl, whisk together balsamic vinegar, soy sauce, olive oil, minced garlic, dried thyme, salt, and black pepper to create the marinade.

Place the cleaned portobello mushroom caps in a shallow dish. Pour the marinade over the mushrooms, ensuring they are well-coated. Let them marinate for about 15-20 minutes.

Grill the marinated portobello mushrooms for approximately 5-7 minutes per side, or until they are tender and have nice grill marks.

During grilling, you can brush the mushrooms with additional marinade for extra flavor.

In the last minute of grilling, you can optionally add a slice of Swiss or provolone cheese on top of each mushroom cap.

Toast the whole-grain burger buns on the grill for a minute or until lightly golden.

Assemble the burgers by spreading Dijon mustard and mayonnaise on the toasted buns.

Place a grilled portobello mushroom cap on each bun.

Top with arugula or baby spinach, tomato slices, and thinly sliced red onion.

Serve the Grilled Portobello Mushroom Burgers hot, accompanied by your favorite side dishes.

Enjoy these hearty and flavorful vegetarian burgers that showcase the rich taste of grilled portobello mushrooms!

Grilled Honey-Lime Chicken Skewers

Ingredients:

For the Marinade:

- 1/4 cup soy sauce
- 3 tablespoons honey
- Juice of 2 limes
- 2 tablespoons olive oil
- 2 cloves garlic, minced
- 1 teaspoon ground cumin
- 1 teaspoon smoked paprika
- Salt and black pepper to taste

For the Chicken Skewers:

- 2 lbs boneless, skinless chicken breasts, cut into 1-inch cubes
- Wooden skewers, soaked in water for 30 minutes
- Zucchini, cherry tomatoes, and bell peppers (for skewering)
- Fresh cilantro, chopped (for garnish)

Instructions:

In a bowl, whisk together soy sauce, honey, lime juice, olive oil, minced garlic, ground cumin, smoked paprika, salt, and black pepper to create the marinade.

Place the chicken cubes in a resealable plastic bag or a shallow dish. Pour the marinade over the chicken, ensuring each piece is well-coated. Marinate in the refrigerator for at least 30 minutes, or preferably 2 hours.

Preheat the grill to medium-high heat.

Thread the marinated chicken cubes and assorted vegetables onto the soaked wooden skewers, alternating for a colorful mix.

Grill the skewers for about 10-12 minutes, turning occasionally, until the chicken is cooked through and has a nice grill marks.

During grilling, you can brush the skewers with any remaining marinade for extra flavor.

Once the skewers are done, transfer them to a serving platter.

Garnish with chopped fresh cilantro for a burst of freshness.

Serve the Grilled Honey-Lime Chicken Skewers hot, accompanied by rice, quinoa, or your favorite side dishes.

Enjoy the delightful combination of sweet honey and zesty lime in these succulent grilled chicken skewers!

Grilled Shrimp Tacos with Avocado Lime Crema

Ingredients:

For the Shrimp Marinade:

- 1 lb large shrimp, peeled and deveined
- 2 tablespoons olive oil
- 2 cloves garlic, minced
- 1 teaspoon ground cumin
- 1 teaspoon smoked paprika
- 1/2 teaspoon chili powder
- Salt and black pepper to taste
- Juice of 1 lime

For the Avocado Lime Crema:

- 1 ripe avocado
- 1/2 cup sour cream
- Juice of 1 lime
- Salt and black pepper to taste

For Assembling Tacos:

- Corn or flour tortillas
- Shredded cabbage or lettuce
- Cherry tomatoes, halved
- Red onion, thinly sliced
- Fresh cilantro, chopped

- Lime wedges (for serving)

Instructions:

In a bowl, combine olive oil, minced garlic, ground cumin, smoked paprika, chili powder, salt, black pepper, and lime juice to create the shrimp marinade.

Toss the peeled and deveined shrimp in the marinade, ensuring each shrimp is well-coated. Let them marinate for about 15-20 minutes.

Preheat the grill to medium-high heat.

Thread the marinated shrimp onto skewers or use a grill basket for easy grilling.

Grill the shrimp for about 2-3 minutes per side, or until they are opaque and have grill marks.

While the shrimp are grilling, prepare the Avocado Lime Crema. In a blender or food processor, combine the ripe avocado, sour cream, lime juice, salt, and black pepper. Blend until smooth and creamy.

Warm the tortillas on the grill for about 10-15 seconds per side.

Assemble the tacos by placing a layer of shredded cabbage or lettuce on each tortilla.

Add grilled shrimp on top, followed by cherry tomatoes, red onion slices, and chopped fresh cilantro.

Drizzle the Avocado Lime Crema over the taco fillings.

Serve the Grilled Shrimp Tacos hot, accompanied by lime wedges on the side.

Enjoy these vibrant and flavorful shrimp tacos with the creamy goodness of avocado lime crema!

Grilled Veggie and Halloumi Quinoa Bowl

Ingredients:

For the Marinade:

- 1/4 cup balsamic vinegar
- 2 tablespoons olive oil
- 2 cloves garlic, minced
- 1 teaspoon dried oregano
- Salt and black pepper to taste

For the Quinoa Bowl:

- 1 cup quinoa, cooked according to package instructions
- 1 zucchini, sliced
- 1 red bell pepper, cut into chunks
- 1 yellow bell pepper, cut into chunks
- 1 red onion, cut into wedges
- 1 cup cherry tomatoes, halved
- 1 block (about 8 oz) halloumi cheese, sliced
- Fresh basil or parsley, chopped (for garnish)

Instructions:

In a bowl, whisk together balsamic vinegar, olive oil, minced garlic, dried oregano, salt, and black pepper to create the marinade.

Place the sliced zucchini, red bell pepper, yellow bell pepper, red onion, and cherry tomatoes in a large bowl. Pour the marinade over the vegetables and toss to coat evenly. Let them marinate for about 15-20 minutes.

Preheat the grill to medium-high heat.

Grill the marinated vegetables and halloumi slices for about 3-4 minutes per side, or until they are tender and have nice grill marks.

While grilling, you can brush the vegetables and halloumi with any remaining marinade for extra flavor.

In a serving bowl, assemble the quinoa bowl by placing a portion of cooked quinoa.

Top the quinoa with grilled vegetables and halloumi slices.

Garnish with chopped fresh basil or parsley for a burst of herbal freshness.

Serve the Grilled Veggie and Halloumi Quinoa Bowl warm, either as a satisfying main dish or a delicious side.

Enjoy this wholesome and nutritious quinoa bowl featuring grilled vegetables and savory halloumi cheese!

Grilled Teriyaki Pineapple Salmon

Ingredients:

For the Teriyaki Marinade:

- 1/4 cup soy sauce
- 3 tablespoons honey
- 2 tablespoons rice vinegar
- 1 tablespoon sesame oil
- 2 cloves garlic, minced
- 1 teaspoon ginger, grated
- 1 tablespoon cornstarch (optional, for thickening)

For the Salmon:

- 4 salmon fillets (about 6 ounces each)
- Salt and black pepper to taste
- 1 large pineapple, peeled, cored, and cut into rings

For Garnish:

- Green onions, chopped
- Sesame seeds
- Fresh cilantro, chopped

Instructions:

In a bowl, whisk together soy sauce, honey, rice vinegar, sesame oil, minced garlic, grated ginger, and cornstarch (if using) to create the teriyaki marinade.

Season the salmon fillets with salt and black pepper. Place the salmon in a shallow dish and pour half of the teriyaki marinade over the fillets. Reserve the remaining marinade for basting.

Marinate the salmon in the refrigerator for at least 30 minutes.

Preheat the grill to medium-high heat.

Grill the pineapple rings for about 2-3 minutes per side, or until they have grill marks. Remove and set aside.

Place the marinated salmon fillets on the grill, skin side down. Grill for about 4-5 minutes per side or until the salmon is cooked through.

During grilling, baste the salmon with the reserved teriyaki marinade for extra flavor.

In the last minute of grilling, place the grilled pineapple rings on the grill to warm them. Remove the salmon and pineapple from the grill.

Serve the Grilled Teriyaki Pineapple Salmon on a platter, topped with chopped green onions, sesame seeds, and fresh cilantro.

Optionally, drizzle any remaining teriyaki marinade over the salmon for added flavor.

Pair with steamed rice or your favorite side dishes.

Enjoy this delightful combination of sweet teriyaki, grilled pineapple, and perfectly cooked salmon!

Grilled Vegetable Stuffed Portobello Mushrooms

Ingredients:

For the Marinade:

- 1/4 cup balsamic vinegar
- 3 tablespoons olive oil
- 2 cloves garlic, minced
- 1 teaspoon dried Italian herbs (oregano, basil, thyme)
- Salt and black pepper to taste

For the Stuffed Portobello Mushrooms:

- 4 large portobello mushroom caps, cleaned and stems removed
- 1 zucchini, diced
- 1 red bell pepper, diced
- 1 yellow bell pepper, diced
- 1 cup cherry tomatoes, halved
- 1 cup fresh spinach, chopped
- 1/2 cup feta cheese, crumbled
- Fresh basil, chopped (for garnish)

Instructions:

In a bowl, whisk together balsamic vinegar, olive oil, minced garlic, dried Italian herbs, salt, and black pepper to create the marinade.

Place the cleaned portobello mushroom caps in a shallow dish. Pour the marinade over the mushrooms, ensuring they are well-coated. Let them marinate for about 15-20 minutes.

Preheat the grill to medium-high heat.

In a mixing bowl, combine diced zucchini, red bell pepper, yellow bell pepper, cherry tomatoes, and chopped spinach.

Remove the portobello mushrooms from the marinade and stuff them with the vegetable mixture.

Place the stuffed mushrooms on the preheated grill and cook for about 5-7 minutes per side, or until the mushrooms are tender and the vegetables are grilled.

During grilling, you can brush the mushrooms with any remaining marinade for extra flavor.

In the last few minutes of grilling, sprinkle crumbled feta cheese over the stuffed mushrooms.

Remove the stuffed portobello mushrooms from the grill.

Garnish with fresh chopped basil for a burst of herbal freshness.

Serve the Grilled Vegetable Stuffed Portobello Mushrooms hot, either as a flavorful appetizer or a satisfying vegetarian main dish.

Enjoy these grilled and stuffed portobello mushrooms with a medley of colorful vegetables and savory feta cheese!

Grilled Lemon-Herb Chicken Drumsticks

Ingredients:

For the Marinade:

- 1/4 cup olive oil
- Zest and juice of 2 lemons
- 3 cloves garlic, minced
- 1 tablespoon fresh rosemary, chopped
- 1 tablespoon fresh thyme leaves
- 1 teaspoon dried oregano
- Salt and black pepper to taste

For the Chicken Drumsticks:

- 12 chicken drumsticks
- Lemon slices (for garnish)
- Fresh parsley, chopped (for garnish)

Instructions:

In a bowl, whisk together olive oil, lemon zest, lemon juice, minced garlic, chopped rosemary, thyme leaves, dried oregano, salt, and black pepper to create the marinade. Place the chicken drumsticks in a large resealable plastic bag or a shallow dish. Pour the marinade over the drumsticks, ensuring they are well-coated. Marinate in the refrigerator for at least 2 hours, or overnight for maximum flavor.

Preheat the grill to medium-high heat.

Remove the chicken drumsticks from the marinade, allowing excess marinade to drip off.

Grill the drumsticks for about 20-25 minutes, turning occasionally, until they are golden brown and cooked through. The internal temperature should reach 165°F (74°C).

During grilling, you can baste the drumsticks with any remaining marinade for extra flavor.

In the last few minutes of grilling, place lemon slices on the grill to get a light char.

Transfer the grilled chicken drumsticks to a serving platter.

Garnish with grilled lemon slices and chopped fresh parsley.

Serve the Grilled Lemon-Herb Chicken Drumsticks hot, accompanied by your favorite side dishes.

Enjoy these juicy and flavorful chicken drumsticks infused with the bright and aromatic combination of lemon and herbs!

Grilled Garlic-Lime Shrimp Tacos

Ingredients:

For the Shrimp Marinade:

- 1 lb large shrimp, peeled and deveined
- 3 tablespoons olive oil
- 4 cloves garlic, minced
- Zest and juice of 2 limes
- 1 teaspoon chili powder
- 1 teaspoon ground cumin
- Salt and black pepper to taste

For the Cabbage Slaw:

- 2 cups shredded green cabbage
- 1 cup shredded purple cabbage
- 1 carrot, julienned
- 2 green onions, thinly sliced
- 1/4 cup fresh cilantro, chopped
- Juice of 1 lime
- 2 tablespoons mayonnaise
- Salt and black pepper to taste

For Assembling Tacos:

- Corn or flour tortillas
- Avocado slices

- Fresh cilantro, chopped (for garnish)
- Lime wedges (for serving)

Instructions:

In a bowl, whisk together olive oil, minced garlic, lime zest, lime juice, chili powder, ground cumin, salt, and black pepper to create the shrimp marinade.

Toss the peeled and deveined shrimp in the marinade, ensuring each shrimp is well-coated. Let them marinate for about 15-20 minutes.

Preheat the grill to medium-high heat.

In a separate bowl, combine shredded green cabbage, shredded purple cabbage, julienned carrot, sliced green onions, chopped cilantro, lime juice, mayonnaise, salt, and black pepper to create the cabbage slaw. Toss until well combined.

Thread the marinated shrimp onto skewers or use a grill basket for easy grilling.

Grill the shrimp for about 2-3 minutes per side, or until they are opaque and have grill marks.

Warm the tortillas on the grill for about 10-15 seconds per side.

Assemble the tacos by placing a layer of cabbage slaw on each tortilla.

Add grilled shrimp on top, followed by avocado slices.

Garnish with fresh chopped cilantro.

Serve the Grilled Garlic-Lime Shrimp Tacos hot, accompanied by lime wedges on the side.

Enjoy these zesty and flavorful shrimp tacos with the vibrant crunch of cabbage slaw!

Grilled Teriyaki Veggie Skewers

Ingredients:

For the Teriyaki Marinade:

- 1/4 cup soy sauce
- 3 tablespoons honey
- 2 tablespoons rice vinegar
- 1 tablespoon sesame oil
- 2 cloves garlic, minced
- 1 teaspoon ginger, grated
- 1 tablespoon cornstarch (optional, for thickening)

For the Veggie Skewers:

- 1 zucchini, sliced into rounds
- 1 yellow bell pepper, cut into chunks
- 1 red bell pepper, cut into chunks
- 1 red onion, cut into wedges
- Cherry tomatoes
- Button mushrooms, cleaned
- Wooden skewers, soaked in water for 30 minutes

Instructions:

In a bowl, whisk together soy sauce, honey, rice vinegar, sesame oil, minced garlic, grated ginger, and cornstarch (if using) to create the teriyaki marinade.

Place the sliced zucchini, yellow bell pepper, red bell pepper, red onion, cherry tomatoes, and button mushrooms in a large bowl. Pour the marinade over the vegetables and toss to coat evenly. Let them marinate for about 15-20 minutes.

Preheat the grill to medium-high heat.

Thread the marinated vegetables onto the soaked wooden skewers, alternating for a colorful mix.

Grill the skewers for about 10-12 minutes, turning occasionally, until the vegetables are tender and have a nice char.

During grilling, you can brush the skewers with any remaining marinade for extra flavor.

Once the veggie skewers are done, transfer them to a serving platter.

Serve the Grilled Teriyaki Veggie Skewers hot, either as a delightful side dish or a satisfying vegetarian main course.

Enjoy the delicious blend of teriyaki flavors and the smokiness from the grill in these vibrant vegetable skewers!

Grilled Peach and Burrata Salad

Ingredients:

For the Balsamic Glaze:

- 1/2 cup balsamic vinegar
- 2 tablespoons honey

For the Salad:

- 4 ripe peaches, halved and pitted
- 1 tablespoon olive oil
- Mixed salad greens (arugula, spinach, or your choice)
- 1 ball of burrata cheese
- Prosciutto slices (optional)
- Balsamic glaze (from the recipe above)
- Fresh basil leaves, torn
- Salt and black pepper to taste

Instructions:

In a small saucepan, combine balsamic vinegar and honey for the balsamic glaze. Bring to a simmer over medium heat, then reduce the heat to low. Simmer for about 10-15 minutes or until the glaze thickens. Remove from heat and let it cool.

Preheat the grill to medium-high heat.

Brush the halved and pitted peaches with olive oil.

Grill the peaches for about 2-3 minutes per side, or until they have grill marks and are slightly softened.

While grilling, you can optionally grill prosciutto slices for a crispy texture.

Arrange the mixed salad greens on a serving platter.

Place the grilled peaches on top of the greens.

Tear the burrata into pieces and distribute it over the salad.

If grilled, arrange crispy prosciutto slices on the salad.

Drizzle the grilled peach and burrata salad with balsamic glaze.

Sprinkle torn fresh basil leaves over the top.

Season with salt and black pepper to taste.

Serve the Grilled Peach and Burrata Salad as a refreshing and elegant appetizer or side dish.

Enjoy the sweet and savory combination of grilled peaches and creamy burrata in this delightful salad!

Grilled Veggie and Pesto Flatbread

Ingredients:

For the Pesto Sauce:

- 2 cups fresh basil leaves, packed
- 1/2 cup grated Parmesan cheese
- 1/3 cup pine nuts
- 2 cloves garlic, minced
- 1/2 cup extra virgin olive oil
- Salt and black pepper to taste

For the Flatbread:

- 4 pieces of flatbread or naan
- 1 zucchini, thinly sliced
- 1 yellow squash, thinly sliced
- 1 red bell pepper, thinly sliced
- 1 red onion, thinly sliced
- 1 cup cherry tomatoes, halved
- 1 cup mozzarella cheese, shredded
- Olive oil for brushing
- Fresh basil leaves (for garnish)

Instructions:

Preheat the grill to medium-high heat.

In a food processor, combine fresh basil, Parmesan cheese, pine nuts, minced garlic, salt, and black pepper. Pulse until finely chopped.

With the food processor running, slowly drizzle in the olive oil until the pesto sauce reaches a smooth consistency. Adjust salt and pepper to taste.

Brush both sides of each flatbread with olive oil.

Place the sliced zucchini, yellow squash, red bell pepper, red onion, and cherry tomatoes in a bowl. Toss the vegetables with a little olive oil, salt, and black pepper.

Grill the flatbreads for about 2 minutes per side, or until they have grill marks and are slightly crispy.

While grilling, add the marinated vegetables to the grill and cook for about 5-7 minutes, turning occasionally, until they are tender and have a nice char.

Spread a generous layer of pesto sauce over each grilled flatbread.

Arrange the grilled vegetables evenly on top of the pesto.

Sprinkle shredded mozzarella cheese over the vegetables.

Close the grill lid and cook for an additional 3-5 minutes, or until the cheese is melted and bubbly.

Remove the flatbreads from the grill and let them cool for a minute.

Garnish with fresh basil leaves.

Slice and serve the Grilled Veggie and Pesto Flatbread as a delicious and colorful appetizer or light meal.

Enjoy this flavorful and vibrant flatbread showcasing the goodness of grilled vegetables and basil pesto!

Grilled Chicken Caesar Salad Wraps

Ingredients:

For the Grilled Chicken:

- 4 boneless, skinless chicken breasts
- 2 tablespoons olive oil
- 1 teaspoon garlic powder
- 1 teaspoon dried oregano
- Salt and black pepper to taste
- Juice of 1 lemon

For the Caesar Dressing:

- 1/2 cup mayonnaise
- 1/4 cup grated Parmesan cheese
- 2 tablespoons Dijon mustard
- 2 cloves garlic, minced
- 1 tablespoon anchovy paste (optional)
- Juice of 1 lemon
- Salt and black pepper to taste

For the Salad Wraps:

- Romaine lettuce leaves
- Cherry tomatoes, halved
- Croutons
- Shaved Parmesan cheese

- Fresh parsley, chopped (for garnish)
- Whole grain or spinach wraps

Instructions:

Preheat the grill to medium-high heat.

In a bowl, mix olive oil, garlic powder, dried oregano, salt, black pepper, and lemon juice to create the marinade.

Coat the chicken breasts with the marinade, ensuring they are well-covered. Let them marinate for at least 30 minutes.

Grill the chicken breasts for about 6-8 minutes per side, or until they are fully cooked with nice grill marks. The internal temperature should reach 165°F (74°C).

While the chicken is grilling, prepare the Caesar dressing by combining mayonnaise, grated Parmesan cheese, Dijon mustard, minced garlic, anchovy paste (if using), lemon juice, salt, and black pepper. Mix until smooth.

Remove the grilled chicken from the grill and let it rest for a few minutes. Slice the chicken into strips.

Assemble the wraps by placing a Romaine lettuce leaf on each wrap.

Add grilled chicken strips, cherry tomatoes, croutons, shaved Parmesan cheese, and a drizzle of Caesar dressing.

Garnish with fresh chopped parsley.

Roll up the wraps and secure them with toothpicks if needed.

Serve the Grilled Chicken Caesar Salad Wraps as a satisfying and flavorful meal.

Enjoy these grilled chicken Caesar salad wraps as a delicious and portable option for a light lunch or dinner!

Grilled Pineapple Chicken Skewers

Ingredients:

For the Marinade:

- 1/4 cup soy sauce
- 3 tablespoons honey
- 2 tablespoons olive oil
- 1 teaspoon garlic powder
- 1 teaspoon ground ginger
- 1 tablespoon rice vinegar
- 1 1/2 lbs boneless, skinless chicken breasts, cut into cubes

For the Skewers:

- Fresh pineapple, cut into chunks
- Bell peppers (assorted colors), cut into chunks
- Red onion, cut into wedges

For Garnish:

- Fresh cilantro, chopped
- Sesame seeds (optional)

Instructions:

In a bowl, whisk together soy sauce, honey, olive oil, garlic powder, ground ginger, and rice vinegar to create the marinade.

Place the chicken cubes in a resealable plastic bag or a shallow dish. Pour half of the marinade over the chicken, reserving the other half for basting. Marinate in the refrigerator for at least 30 minutes.

Preheat the grill to medium-high heat.

Thread the marinated chicken cubes, pineapple chunks, bell pepper chunks, and red onion wedges onto skewers, alternating for a colorful mix.

Grill the skewers for about 10-12 minutes, turning occasionally, until the chicken is cooked through and has a nice char.

During grilling, baste the skewers with the reserved marinade for extra flavor.

Once the skewers are done, transfer them to a serving platter.

Garnish with chopped fresh cilantro and sesame seeds (if using).

Serve the Grilled Pineapple Chicken Skewers hot, either as an appetizer or a main course.

Enjoy the sweet and savory combination of grilled pineapple and tender chicken in these delightful skewers!

Grilled Eggplant and Mozzarella Stacks

Ingredients:

For the Balsamic Glaze:

- 1/2 cup balsamic vinegar
- 2 tablespoons honey

For the Eggplant Stacks:

- 2 large eggplants, sliced into rounds
- Olive oil for brushing
- Salt and black pepper to taste
- 1 cup fresh mozzarella, sliced
- 1 cup cherry tomatoes, halved
- Fresh basil leaves
- Balsamic glaze (from the recipe above)

Instructions:

Preheat the grill to medium-high heat.

In a small saucepan, combine balsamic vinegar and honey for the balsamic glaze. Bring to a simmer over medium heat, then reduce the heat to low. Simmer for about 10-15 minutes or until the glaze thickens. Remove from heat and let it cool.

Brush the eggplant slices with olive oil and season with salt and black pepper.

Grill the eggplant slices for about 2-3 minutes per side, or until they have grill marks and are tender.

While grilling, place mozzarella slices on the eggplant slices for the last minute of cooking to allow them to melt slightly.

Remove the grilled eggplant slices from the grill and let them cool for a minute.

Assemble the stacks by layering grilled eggplant, fresh mozzarella, cherry tomatoes, and fresh basil leaves.

Drizzle the stacks with balsamic glaze.

Repeat the layering process to create multiple stacks.

Serve the Grilled Eggplant and Mozzarella Stacks as an elegant and flavorful appetizer or side dish.

Enjoy these delicious and visually appealing eggplant and mozzarella stacks with the rich flavor of balsamic glaze!

Grilled Teriyaki Salmon Bowls

Ingredients:

For the Teriyaki Marinade:

- 1/4 cup soy sauce
- 3 tablespoons honey
- 2 tablespoons mirin (sweet rice wine)
- 1 tablespoon rice vinegar
- 1 tablespoon sesame oil
- 2 cloves garlic, minced
- 1 teaspoon ginger, grated
- 1 tablespoon cornstarch (optional, for thickening)

For the Grilled Salmon:

- 4 salmon fillets (about 6 ounces each)
- Salt and black pepper to taste
- Sesame seeds (for garnish)

For the Bowls:

- Cooked white or brown rice
- Steamed broccoli florets
- Sliced carrots
- Avocado slices
- Green onions, sliced
- Sesame seeds (for garnish)

Instructions:

In a bowl, whisk together soy sauce, honey, mirin, rice vinegar, sesame oil, minced garlic, grated ginger, and cornstarch (if using) to create the teriyaki marinade.

Season the salmon fillets with salt and black pepper. Place the salmon in a shallow dish and pour half of the teriyaki marinade over the fillets. Reserve the remaining marinade for basting. Marinate in the refrigerator for at least 30 minutes.

Preheat the grill to medium-high heat.

Remove the salmon fillets from the marinade, allowing excess marinade to drip off.

Grill the salmon for about 4-5 minutes per side, or until the salmon is cooked through and has a nice char. Baste with the reserved marinade during grilling for extra flavor.

While the salmon is grilling, prepare the rice and steam the broccoli florets.

Assemble the bowls by placing a serving of cooked rice in each bowl.

Top with grilled teriyaki salmon fillets.

Add steamed broccoli, sliced carrots, avocado slices, and green onions.

Drizzle any remaining teriyaki marinade over the bowls.

Garnish with sesame seeds.

Serve the Grilled Teriyaki Salmon Bowls hot, offering a balance of flavors and textures.

Enjoy these delicious and nutritious teriyaki salmon bowls for a satisfying and wholesome meal!

Grilled Halloumi and Vegetable Skewers

Ingredients:

For the Marinade:

- 1/4 cup olive oil
- Juice of 1 lemon
- 2 cloves garlic, minced
- 1 teaspoon dried oregano
- Salt and black pepper to taste

For the Skewers:

- 1 block halloumi cheese, cut into cubes
- Cherry tomatoes
- Zucchini, sliced into rounds
- Red bell pepper, cut into chunks
- Red onion, cut into wedges
- Wooden skewers, soaked in water for 30 minutes

For Garnish:

- Fresh parsley, chopped
- Lemon wedges

Instructions:

In a bowl, whisk together olive oil, lemon juice, minced garlic, dried oregano, salt, and black pepper to create the marinade.

Cut the halloumi cheese into cubes.

Place the halloumi cubes, cherry tomatoes, zucchini rounds, red bell pepper chunks, and red onion wedges in a large bowl. Pour the marinade over the ingredients and toss gently to coat. Let them marinate for about 15-20 minutes.

Preheat the grill to medium-high heat.

Thread the marinated halloumi cubes and vegetables onto the soaked wooden skewers, alternating for a colorful mix.

Grill the skewers for about 8-10 minutes, turning occasionally, until the halloumi is golden and the vegetables are tender with a nice char.

During grilling, you can brush the skewers with any remaining marinade for extra flavor.

Once the skewers are done, transfer them to a serving platter.

Garnish with freshly chopped parsley.

Serve the Grilled Halloumi and Vegetable Skewers hot, accompanied by lemon wedges on the side.

Enjoy these flavorful and satisfying grilled halloumi and vegetable skewers as a delicious appetizer or a delightful vegetarian main course!

Grilled Chimichurri Steak Tacos

Ingredients:

For the Chimichurri Sauce:

- 1 cup fresh parsley, chopped
- 1/4 cup fresh cilantro, chopped
- 4 cloves garlic, minced
- 1/2 cup red wine vinegar
- 1/2 cup extra virgin olive oil
- 1 teaspoon dried oregano
- 1 teaspoon red pepper flakes (adjust to taste)
- Salt and black pepper to taste

For the Grilled Steak:

- 1.5 lbs flank steak
- Salt and black pepper to taste
- Corn or flour tortillas

For Toppings:

- Sliced red onion
- Sliced tomatoes
- Avocado slices
- Lime wedges
- Fresh cilantro, chopped

Instructions:

In a bowl, combine chopped parsley, chopped cilantro, minced garlic, red wine vinegar, olive oil, dried oregano, red pepper flakes, salt, and black pepper to create the chimichurri sauce. Mix well and set aside.

Season the flank steak with salt and black pepper.

Preheat the grill to medium-high heat.

Grill the steak for about 4-5 minutes per side, or until it reaches your desired level of doneness.

Remove the steak from the grill and let it rest for a few minutes.

Slice the grilled steak thinly against the grain.

Warm the tortillas on the grill for about 10-15 seconds per side.

Assemble the tacos by placing a portion of sliced grilled steak on each tortilla.

Top with chimichurri sauce, sliced red onion, sliced tomatoes, avocado slices, and chopped cilantro.

Squeeze fresh lime juice over the top.

Serve the Grilled Chimichurri Steak Tacos hot, offering a burst of flavors and textures.

Enjoy these delicious and zesty chimichurri steak tacos for a memorable and satisfying meal!

Grilled Vegetable and Quinoa Stuffed Bell Peppers

Ingredients:

For the Quinoa:

- 1 cup quinoa, rinsed
- 2 cups vegetable broth
- 1 teaspoon olive oil
- Salt and black pepper to taste

For the Grilled Vegetables:

- 1 zucchini, sliced
- 1 yellow squash, sliced
- 1 red bell pepper, cut into chunks
- 1 red onion, cut into wedges
- Cherry tomatoes, halved
- 2 tablespoons olive oil
- 1 teaspoon dried Italian herbs (oregano, basil, thyme)
- Salt and black pepper to taste

For the Stuffed Bell Peppers:

- 4 large bell peppers, halved and seeds removed
- 1 cup feta cheese, crumbled
- Fresh parsley, chopped (for garnish)

Instructions:

In a medium saucepan, combine quinoa, vegetable broth, olive oil, salt, and black pepper. Bring to a boil, then reduce heat to low, cover, and simmer for 15-20 minutes or until quinoa is cooked and liquid is absorbed.

Preheat the grill to medium-high heat.

In a large bowl, toss the sliced zucchini, yellow squash, red bell pepper chunks, red onion wedges, and cherry tomatoes with olive oil, dried Italian herbs, salt, and black pepper.

Grill the vegetables for about 8-10 minutes, turning occasionally, until they are tender and have nice grill marks.

While grilling, brush the bell pepper halves with a little olive oil and grill them for about 2-3 minutes per side.

In a mixing bowl, combine the cooked quinoa with the grilled vegetables. Stir in crumbled feta cheese.

Preheat the grill to medium heat.

Stuff each grilled bell pepper half with the quinoa and vegetable mixture.

Grill the stuffed bell peppers for an additional 5-7 minutes, or until they are heated through.

Remove the stuffed bell peppers from the grill and garnish with fresh chopped parsley.

Serve the Grilled Vegetable and Quinoa Stuffed Bell Peppers warm, offering a nutritious and flavorful meal.

Enjoy these vibrant and delicious stuffed bell peppers with a delightful combination of quinoa, grilled vegetables, and feta cheese!

Grilled Honey-Lime Chicken Skewers

Ingredients:

For the Marinade:

- 1/4 cup soy sauce
- 3 tablespoons honey
- Zest and juice of 2 limes
- 2 tablespoons olive oil
- 2 cloves garlic, minced
- 1 teaspoon ground cumin
- 1 teaspoon paprika
- Salt and black pepper to taste

For the Chicken Skewers:

- 1.5 lbs boneless, skinless chicken breasts, cut into cubes
- Bell peppers (assorted colors), cut into chunks
- Red onion, cut into wedges
- Wooden skewers, soaked in water for 30 minutes

For Garnish:

- Fresh cilantro, chopped
- Lime wedges

Instructions:

In a bowl, whisk together soy sauce, honey, lime zest, lime juice, olive oil, minced garlic, ground cumin, paprika, salt, and black pepper to create the marinade.

Place the chicken cubes in a resealable plastic bag or a shallow dish. Pour half of the marinade over the chicken, reserving the other half for basting. Marinate in the refrigerator for at least 30 minutes.

Preheat the grill to medium-high heat.

Thread the marinated chicken cubes, bell pepper chunks, and red onion wedges onto the soaked wooden skewers, alternating for a colorful mix.

Grill the skewers for about 10-12 minutes, turning occasionally, until the chicken is cooked through and has a nice char.

During grilling, baste the skewers with the reserved marinade for extra flavor.

Once the skewers are done, transfer them to a serving platter.

Garnish with freshly chopped cilantro.

Serve the Grilled Honey-Lime Chicken Skewers hot, accompanied by lime wedges on the side.

Enjoy these succulent and flavorful honey-lime chicken skewers for a delightful and satisfying meal!

Grilled Portobello Mushroom Burgers

Ingredients:

For the Marinade:

- 1/4 cup balsamic vinegar
- 2 tablespoons soy sauce
- 2 tablespoons olive oil
- 2 cloves garlic, minced
- 1 teaspoon dried thyme
- Salt and black pepper to taste

For the Portobello Mushrooms:

- 4 large portobello mushroom caps, cleaned and stems removed
- Buns for serving
- Goat cheese or feta cheese (optional)
- Arugula or spinach leaves
- Sliced tomatoes
- Red onion, thinly sliced
- Avocado slices
- Dijon mustard or your favorite burger sauce

Instructions:

> In a bowl, whisk together balsamic vinegar, soy sauce, olive oil, minced garlic, dried thyme, salt, and black pepper to create the marinade.

Place the cleaned portobello mushroom caps in a shallow dish. Pour the marinade over the mushrooms, ensuring they are well-coated. Let them marinate for about 15-20 minutes.

Preheat the grill to medium-high heat.

Grill the marinated portobello mushrooms for about 4-5 minutes per side, or until they are tender and have grill marks.

During grilling, you can brush the mushrooms with any remaining marinade for extra flavor.

While the mushrooms are grilling, prepare the burger toppings: slice tomatoes, red onion, and avocado. Get the buns ready.

Optional: Spread goat cheese or feta cheese on the grilled mushroom caps during the last minute of grilling.

Assemble the burgers by placing a grilled portobello mushroom on each bun.

Top with arugula or spinach leaves, sliced tomatoes, red onion, avocado slices, and your favorite burger sauce or Dijon mustard.

Serve the Grilled Portobello Mushroom Burgers hot, offering a delicious and satisfying vegetarian option.

Enjoy these flavorful and hearty grilled portobello mushroom burgers as a tasty alternative to traditional meat-based burgers!

Grilled Veggie Quesadillas with Cilantro Lime Crema

Ingredients:

For the Veggie Filling:

- 1 zucchini, sliced
- 1 yellow squash, sliced
- 1 red bell pepper, sliced
- 1 red onion, thinly sliced
- 1 cup corn kernels (fresh or frozen)
- 2 tablespoons olive oil
- 1 teaspoon ground cumin
- 1 teaspoon chili powder
- Salt and black pepper to taste

For the Cilantro Lime Crema:

- 1/2 cup sour cream
- 2 tablespoons fresh cilantro, chopped
- Zest and juice of 1 lime
- Salt and black pepper to taste

For the Quesadillas:

- Flour tortillas
- Shredded Monterey Jack or Mexican blend cheese
- Avocado slices (optional)

Instructions:

Preheat the grill to medium-high heat.

In a bowl, toss zucchini, yellow squash, red bell pepper, red onion, and corn kernels with olive oil, ground cumin, chili powder, salt, and black pepper.

Grill the vegetables for about 8-10 minutes, turning occasionally, until they are tender and have a nice char.

While grilling, prepare the cilantro lime crema by mixing sour cream, chopped cilantro, lime zest, lime juice, salt, and black pepper in a small bowl. Set aside.

Place a flour tortilla on the grill and sprinkle a layer of shredded cheese on half of the tortilla.

Spoon a generous portion of the grilled veggie filling over the cheese.

Add optional avocado slices on top of the veggies.

Fold the tortilla in half, creating a quesadilla.

Grill the quesadilla for about 2-3 minutes per side, or until the cheese is melted and the tortilla has grill marks.

Repeat the process for additional quesadillas.

Once the quesadillas are done, remove them from the grill and let them cool for a minute.

Serve the Grilled Veggie Quesadillas with Cilantro Lime Crema on the side for dipping.

Enjoy these flavorful and grilled veggie quesadillas as a delicious and satisfying meal or snack!

Grilled Lemon-Garlic Shrimp Skewers

Ingredients:

For the Marinade:

- 1/4 cup olive oil
- Zest and juice of 2 lemons
- 4 cloves garlic, minced
- 1 tablespoon fresh parsley, chopped
- 1 teaspoon paprika
- 1 teaspoon dried oregano
- Salt and black pepper to taste

For the Shrimp Skewers:

- 1.5 lbs large shrimp, peeled and deveined
- Lemon slices (for garnish)
- Fresh parsley, chopped (for garnish)

Instructions:

In a bowl, whisk together olive oil, lemon zest, lemon juice, minced garlic, chopped fresh parsley, paprika, dried oregano, salt, and black pepper to create the marinade.

Place the peeled and deveined shrimp in a large resealable plastic bag or a shallow dish.

Pour the marinade over the shrimp, ensuring they are well-coated. Marinate in the refrigerator for about 15-20 minutes.

Preheat the grill to medium-high heat.

Thread the marinated shrimp onto skewers, ensuring they are evenly distributed.

Grill the shrimp skewers for about 2-3 minutes per side, or until the shrimp are opaque and have nice grill marks.

During grilling, you can baste the shrimp with any remaining marinade for extra flavor.

In the last few minutes of grilling, place lemon slices on the grill to get a light char.

Remove the shrimp skewers from the grill and transfer them to a serving platter.

Garnish with grilled lemon slices and chopped fresh parsley.

Serve the Grilled Lemon-Garlic Shrimp Skewers hot, accompanied by your favorite side dishes.

Enjoy these delicious and aromatic grilled lemon-garlic shrimp skewers for a quick and flavorful seafood dish!

Grilled Teriyaki Pineapple Chicken Skewers

Ingredients:

For the Teriyaki Marinade:

- 1/4 cup soy sauce
- 3 tablespoons honey
- 2 tablespoons rice vinegar
- 1 tablespoon sesame oil
- 2 cloves garlic, minced
- 1 teaspoon ginger, grated
- 1 tablespoon cornstarch (optional, for thickening)

For the Chicken Skewers:

- 1.5 lbs boneless, skinless chicken thighs, cut into cubes
- Fresh pineapple, cut into chunks
- Bell peppers (assorted colors), cut into chunks
- Red onion, cut into wedges
- Wooden skewers, soaked in water for 30 minutes

For Garnish:

- Sesame seeds
- Green onions, sliced

Instructions:

In a bowl, whisk together soy sauce, honey, rice vinegar, sesame oil, minced garlic, grated ginger, and cornstarch (if using) to create the teriyaki marinade.

Place the chicken cubes in a resealable plastic bag or a shallow dish. Pour half of the marinade over the chicken, reserving the other half for basting. Marinate in the refrigerator for at least 30 minutes.

Preheat the grill to medium-high heat.

Thread the marinated chicken cubes, pineapple chunks, bell pepper chunks, and red onion wedges onto the soaked wooden skewers, alternating for a colorful mix.

Grill the skewers for about 10-12 minutes, turning occasionally, until the chicken is cooked through and has a nice char.

During grilling, baste the skewers with the reserved marinade for extra flavor.

Once the skewers are done, transfer them to a serving platter.

Garnish with sesame seeds and sliced green onions.

Serve the Grilled Teriyaki Pineapple Chicken Skewers hot, either as an appetizer or a main course.

Enjoy the delightful combination of teriyaki-marinated chicken and sweet grilled pineapple in these flavorful skewers!

Grilled Caprese Stuffed Portobello Mushrooms

Ingredients:

For the Balsamic Glaze:

- 1/2 cup balsamic vinegar
- 2 tablespoons honey

For the Stuffed Portobello Mushrooms:

- 4 large portobello mushroom caps, cleaned and stems removed
- 2 tablespoons olive oil
- 4 cloves garlic, minced
- Salt and black pepper to taste

For the Caprese Filling:

- 1 cup cherry tomatoes, halved
- 1 cup fresh mozzarella balls (or cubed mozzarella)
- Fresh basil leaves, torn
- Balsamic glaze (from the recipe above)

Instructions:

In a small saucepan, combine balsamic vinegar and honey for the balsamic glaze. Bring to a simmer over medium heat, then reduce the heat to low. Simmer for about 10-15 minutes or until the glaze thickens. Remove from heat and let it cool.

Preheat the grill to medium-high heat.

Clean the portobello mushroom caps and remove the stems.

In a small bowl, mix olive oil, minced garlic, salt, and black pepper. Brush the inside and outside of the mushroom caps with this mixture.

Grill the mushroom caps for about 3-4 minutes per side, or until they are slightly softened and have grill marks.

While grilling, prepare the caprese filling by combining cherry tomatoes, fresh mozzarella, and torn basil leaves in a bowl.

Once the mushroom caps are grilled, fill each cap with the caprese mixture.

Drizzle the stuffed mushrooms with balsamic glaze.

Close the grill lid and cook for an additional 3-5 minutes, or until the cheese is melted and bubbly.

Remove the stuffed mushrooms from the grill and transfer them to a serving platter.

Drizzle with more balsamic glaze for added flavor.

Serve the Grilled Caprese Stuffed Portobello Mushrooms warm, offering a delightful and elegant appetizer or side dish.

Enjoy the rich and savory flavors of these grilled caprese stuffed portobello mushrooms!

Grilled Lemon Herb Salmon

Ingredients:

For the Marinade:

- 1/4 cup olive oil
- Zest and juice of 2 lemons
- 2 tablespoons fresh parsley, chopped
- 1 tablespoon fresh dill, chopped
- 2 cloves garlic, minced
- Salt and black pepper to taste

For the Salmon:

- 4 salmon fillets (about 6 ounces each)
- Lemon slices (for garnish)

Instructions:

In a bowl, whisk together olive oil, lemon zest, lemon juice, chopped fresh parsley, chopped fresh dill, minced garlic, salt, and black pepper to create the marinade.
Place the salmon fillets in a shallow dish. Pour the marinade over the salmon, ensuring they are well-coated. Marinate in the refrigerator for about 15-20 minutes.
Preheat the grill to medium-high heat.
Remove the salmon fillets from the marinade, allowing excess marinade to drip off.
Grill the salmon for about 4-5 minutes per side, or until the salmon is cooked through and easily flakes with a fork.

During grilling, you can place lemon slices on the grill for a few seconds to get a light char.

Once the salmon is done, transfer the fillets to a serving platter.

Garnish with grilled lemon slices.

Serve the Grilled Lemon Herb Salmon hot, accompanied by your favorite side dishes.

Enjoy this light and flavorful grilled lemon herb salmon for a healthy and delicious meal!

Grilled Vegetable and Pesto Pasta Salad

Ingredients:

For the Pesto Sauce:

- 2 cups fresh basil leaves, packed
- 1/2 cup grated Parmesan cheese
- 1/3 cup pine nuts
- 2 cloves garlic, minced
- 1/2 cup extra virgin olive oil
- Salt and black pepper to taste

For the Grilled Vegetables:

- 1 zucchini, sliced
- 1 yellow squash, sliced
- 1 red bell pepper, cut into chunks
- 1 red onion, cut into wedges
- Cherry tomatoes, halved
- 2 tablespoons olive oil
- Salt and black pepper to taste

For the Pasta Salad:

- 1 lb fusilli or your favorite pasta, cooked al dente
- 1 cup mozzarella cheese, cubed
- 1/2 cup Kalamata olives, sliced
- Fresh basil leaves, torn

- Balsamic glaze (optional, for drizzling)

Instructions:

Preheat the grill to medium-high heat.

In a food processor, combine fresh basil, Parmesan cheese, pine nuts, minced garlic, salt, and black pepper. Pulse until finely chopped.

With the food processor running, slowly drizzle in the olive oil until the pesto sauce reaches a smooth consistency. Adjust salt and pepper to taste.

Place zucchini, yellow squash, red bell pepper, red onion, and cherry tomatoes in a bowl. Toss the vegetables with olive oil, salt, and black pepper.

Grill the vegetables for about 8-10 minutes, turning occasionally, until they are tender and have a nice char.

While grilling, cook the pasta according to package instructions. Drain and let it cool.

In a large bowl, combine the grilled vegetables, cooked pasta, mozzarella cheese, Kalamata olives, and torn basil leaves.

Add the prepared pesto sauce to the bowl and toss everything together until well coated.

Drizzle with balsamic glaze if desired.

Serve the Grilled Vegetable and Pesto Pasta Salad at room temperature or chilled.

Enjoy this vibrant and flavorful pasta salad featuring grilled vegetables and a delightful basil pesto!

Grilled Teriyaki Tofu Skewers

Ingredients:

For the Teriyaki Marinade:

- 1/4 cup soy sauce
- 3 tablespoons honey
- 2 tablespoons mirin (sweet rice wine)
- 1 tablespoon rice vinegar
- 1 tablespoon sesame oil
- 2 cloves garlic, minced
- 1 teaspoon ginger, grated
- 1 tablespoon cornstarch (optional, for thickening)

For the Tofu Skewers:

- 1 block extra-firm tofu, pressed and cut into cubes
- Bell peppers (assorted colors), cut into chunks
- Red onion, cut into wedges
- Pineapple chunks
- Wooden skewers, soaked in water for 30 minutes

For Garnish:

- Sesame seeds
- Green onions, sliced

Instructions:

In a bowl, whisk together soy sauce, honey, mirin, rice vinegar, sesame oil, minced garlic, grated ginger, and cornstarch (if using) to create the teriyaki marinade.

Press the tofu to remove excess water, then cut it into cubes.

Place the tofu cubes in a resealable plastic bag or a shallow dish. Pour half of the teriyaki marinade over the tofu, reserving the other half for basting. Marinate in the refrigerator for at least 30 minutes.

Preheat the grill to medium-high heat.

Thread the marinated tofu cubes, bell pepper chunks, red onion wedges, and pineapple chunks onto the soaked wooden skewers, alternating for a colorful mix.

Grill the skewers for about 10-12 minutes, turning occasionally, until the tofu is lightly browned and the vegetables are tender.

During grilling, baste the skewers with the reserved marinade for extra flavor.

Once the skewers are done, transfer them to a serving platter.

Garnish with sesame seeds and sliced green onions.

Serve the Grilled Teriyaki Tofu Skewers hot, either as an appetizer or a main course.

Enjoy these delicious and flavorful teriyaki tofu skewers as a tasty vegetarian option for your grill!

Grilled Southwest Chicken Salad

Ingredients:

For the Southwest Chicken Marinade:

- 1/4 cup olive oil
- Juice of 2 limes
- 1 teaspoon ground cumin
- 1 teaspoon chili powder
- 1 teaspoon smoked paprika
- 2 cloves garlic, minced
- Salt and black pepper to taste

For the Grilled Chicken:

- 1.5 lbs boneless, skinless chicken breasts

For the Salad:

- Mixed salad greens
- Black beans, drained and rinsed
- Corn kernels (fresh or thawed if frozen)
- Cherry tomatoes, halved
- Avocado slices
- Red onion, thinly sliced
- Fresh cilantro, chopped
- Tortilla strips or crushed tortilla chips (optional, for crunch)

For the Chipotle Lime Dressing:

- 1/4 cup mayonnaise
- 2 tablespoons Greek yogurt
- Juice of 1 lime
- 1 tablespoon adobo sauce from canned chipotle peppers
- Salt and black pepper to taste

Instructions:

In a bowl, whisk together olive oil, lime juice, ground cumin, chili powder, smoked paprika, minced garlic, salt, and black pepper to create the Southwest chicken marinade.

Place the chicken breasts in a resealable plastic bag or a shallow dish. Pour the marinade over the chicken, ensuring they are well-coated. Marinate in the refrigerator for at least 30 minutes.

Preheat the grill to medium-high heat.

Grill the chicken for about 6-8 minutes per side, or until the internal temperature reaches 165°F (74°C) and the chicken is cooked through with a nice char.

While the chicken is grilling, prepare the salad ingredients and the chipotle lime dressing.

For the chipotle lime dressing, whisk together mayonnaise, Greek yogurt, lime juice, adobo sauce, salt, and black pepper. Adjust the seasonings to taste.

Once the chicken is done, let it rest for a few minutes before slicing it into strips.

In a large bowl, assemble the salad by combining mixed greens, black beans, corn, cherry tomatoes, avocado slices, red onion, and chopped cilantro.

Top the salad with grilled Southwest chicken strips.

Drizzle the chipotle lime dressing over the salad.

Optional: Sprinkle tortilla strips or crushed tortilla chips on top for added crunch.

Toss the salad gently to combine all the flavors.

Serve the Grilled Southwest Chicken Salad immediately, offering a fresh and flavorful meal.

Enjoy this hearty and satisfying Southwest chicken salad with a zesty chipotle lime dressing!

Grilled Peach and Halloumi Salad

Ingredients:

For the Grilled Peaches:

- 4 ripe peaches, halved and pitted
- 1 tablespoon honey
- 1 tablespoon olive oil

For the Grilled Halloumi:

- 1 block halloumi cheese, sliced

For the Salad:

- Mixed salad greens (arugula, spinach, or your choice)
- Cherry tomatoes, halved
- Red onion, thinly sliced
- Fresh basil leaves, torn

For the Balsamic Glaze:

- 1/2 cup balsamic vinegar
- 2 tablespoons honey

For Garnish:

- Pomegranate seeds (optional)
- Candied pecans or walnuts (optional)

Instructions:

Preheat the grill to medium-high heat.

In a small bowl, mix honey and olive oil. Brush the cut sides of the peaches with this mixture.

Grill the peaches for about 2-3 minutes per side, or until they have grill marks and are slightly softened.

While grilling, place halloumi cheese slices on the grill and cook for about 1-2 minutes per side, or until they are golden brown and have grill marks.

In a small saucepan, combine balsamic vinegar and honey for the balsamic glaze. Bring to a simmer over medium heat, then reduce the heat to low. Simmer for about 10-15 minutes or until the glaze thickens. Remove from heat and let it cool.

In a large salad bowl, combine mixed greens, cherry tomatoes, thinly sliced red onion, and torn basil leaves.

Arrange the grilled peaches and halloumi slices over the salad.

Optional: Sprinkle pomegranate seeds and candied pecans or walnuts for added texture and flavor.

Drizzle the balsamic glaze over the salad just before serving.

Toss the salad gently to combine all the ingredients.

Serve the Grilled Peach and Halloumi Salad immediately, offering a refreshing and summery dish.

Enjoy this delightful grilled peach and halloumi salad with a perfect balance of sweet and savory flavors!

Grilled Cilantro-Lime Chicken Tacos

Ingredients:

For the Cilantro-Lime Marinade:

- 1/4 cup olive oil
- Juice of 3 limes
- 2 tablespoons fresh cilantro, chopped
- 2 cloves garlic, minced
- 1 teaspoon ground cumin
- 1 teaspoon chili powder
- Salt and black pepper to taste

For the Grilled Chicken:

- 1.5 lbs boneless, skinless chicken thighs

For the Tacos:

- Corn or flour tortillas
- Shredded lettuce
- Diced tomatoes
- Red onion, finely chopped
- Jalapeño slices (optional)
- Sour cream or Greek yogurt
- Fresh cilantro, chopped
- Lime wedges

Instructions:

In a bowl, whisk together olive oil, lime juice, chopped cilantro, minced garlic, ground cumin, chili powder, salt, and black pepper to create the cilantro-lime marinade.

Place the chicken thighs in a resealable plastic bag or a shallow dish. Pour the marinade over the chicken, ensuring they are well-coated. Marinate in the refrigerator for at least 30 minutes.

Preheat the grill to medium-high heat.

Grill the chicken thighs for about 6-8 minutes per side, or until the internal temperature reaches 165°F (74°C) and the chicken is cooked through with a nice char.

While the chicken is grilling, warm the tortillas on the grill for about 10-15 seconds per side.

Remove the chicken from the grill and let it rest for a few minutes before slicing it into strips.

Assemble the tacos by placing a portion of grilled cilantro-lime chicken on each tortilla. Top with shredded lettuce, diced tomatoes, finely chopped red onion, jalapeño slices (if using), and a dollop of sour cream or Greek yogurt.

Sprinkle fresh chopped cilantro over the top.

Serve the Grilled Cilantro-Lime Chicken Tacos hot, accompanied by lime wedges on the side.

Enjoy these flavorful and zesty grilled cilantro-lime chicken tacos for a delicious and satisfying meal!

Grilled Teriyaki Pineapple Shrimp Skewers

Ingredients:

For the Teriyaki Marinade:

- 1/4 cup soy sauce
- 3 tablespoons honey
- 2 tablespoons rice vinegar
- 1 tablespoon sesame oil
- 2 cloves garlic, minced
- 1 teaspoon ginger, grated
- 1 tablespoon cornstarch (optional, for thickening)

For the Shrimp Skewers:

- 1.5 lbs large shrimp, peeled and deveined
- Fresh pineapple, cut into chunks
- Red and yellow bell peppers, cut into chunks
- Red onion, cut into wedges
- Wooden skewers, soaked in water for 30 minutes

For Garnish:

- Green onions, sliced
- Sesame seeds

Instructions:

In a bowl, whisk together soy sauce, honey, rice vinegar, sesame oil, minced garlic, grated ginger, and cornstarch (if using) to create the teriyaki marinade.

Place the peeled and deveined shrimp in a resealable plastic bag or a shallow dish. Pour half of the teriyaki marinade over the shrimp, reserving the other half for basting.

Marinate in the refrigerator for about 30 minutes.

Preheat the grill to medium-high heat.

Thread the marinated shrimp, pineapple chunks, bell pepper chunks, and red onion wedges onto the soaked wooden skewers, alternating for a colorful mix.

Grill the skewers for about 8-10 minutes, turning occasionally, until the shrimp are opaque and have a nice char.

During grilling, baste the skewers with the reserved marinade for extra flavor.

Once the skewers are done, transfer them to a serving platter.

Garnish with sliced green onions and sprinkle sesame seeds over the top.

Serve the Grilled Teriyaki Pineapple Shrimp Skewers hot, either as an appetizer or a main course.

Enjoy the sweet and savory flavors of these teriyaki pineapple shrimp skewers for a delightful and easy-to-make dish!

Grilled Vegetable and Hummus Wrap

Ingredients:

For the Grilled Vegetables:

- 1 zucchini, sliced
- 1 yellow squash, sliced
- 1 red bell pepper, sliced
- 1 red onion, thinly sliced
- Cherry tomatoes, halved
- 2 tablespoons olive oil
- 1 teaspoon dried oregano
- Salt and black pepper to taste

For the Hummus Spread:

- 1 cup hummus (store-bought or homemade)
- Juice of 1 lemon
- 2 cloves garlic, minced
- Fresh parsley, chopped (for garnish)

Additional Ingredients:

- Whole wheat or spinach tortillas
- Fresh spinach leaves
- Feta cheese, crumbled (optional)

Instructions:

Preheat the grill to medium-high heat.

In a bowl, toss zucchini, yellow squash, red bell pepper, red onion, and cherry tomatoes with olive oil, dried oregano, salt, and black pepper.

Grill the vegetables for about 8-10 minutes, turning occasionally, until they are tender and have a nice char.

While grilling, prepare the hummus spread by combining hummus, lemon juice, and minced garlic in a bowl. Mix well.

Once the vegetables are done, remove them from the grill and set aside.

Warm the tortillas on the grill for about 10-15 seconds per side.

Spread a generous layer of hummus mixture onto each tortilla.

Arrange a handful of fresh spinach leaves on top of the hummus.

Place a portion of the grilled vegetables on one side of the tortilla.

Optional: Sprinkle crumbled feta cheese over the vegetables.

Garnish with fresh chopped parsley.

Fold the tortilla, creating a wrap.

Repeat the process for additional wraps.

Serve the Grilled Vegetable and Hummus Wraps warm, offering a flavorful and wholesome meal.

Enjoy these delicious and nutritious grilled vegetable and hummus wraps as a satisfying lunch or dinner option!

Grilled Salmon with Lemon-Dill Butter

Ingredients:

For the Lemon-Dill Butter:

- 1/2 cup unsalted butter, softened
- Zest of 1 lemon
- 2 tablespoons fresh dill, chopped
- 1 tablespoon lemon juice
- Salt and black pepper to taste

For the Grilled Salmon:

- 4 salmon fillets (about 6 ounces each)
- Olive oil for brushing
- Salt and black pepper to taste

For Garnish:

- Fresh dill sprigs
- Lemon wedges

Instructions:

In a bowl, combine softened butter, lemon zest, chopped fresh dill, lemon juice, salt, and black pepper. Mix well to create the lemon-dill butter. Set aside.

Preheat the grill to medium-high heat.

Brush the salmon fillets with olive oil and season with salt and black pepper.

Place the salmon fillets on the grill and cook for about 4-5 minutes per side, or until the salmon is cooked through and has grill marks.

During the last minute of grilling, add a dollop of lemon-dill butter on top of each salmon fillet.

Close the grill lid and let the butter melt over the salmon.

Once the salmon is done, transfer it to a serving platter.

Garnish with fresh dill sprigs and lemon wedges.

Serve the Grilled Salmon with Lemon-Dill Butter hot, accompanied by your favorite side dishes.

Enjoy this simple yet elegant grilled salmon with the delightful flavors of lemon and dill-infused butter!

Grilled Vegetable Quinoa Bowl with Avocado-Lime Dressing

Ingredients:

For the Grilled Vegetables:

- 1 zucchini, sliced
- 1 yellow squash, sliced
- 1 red bell pepper, sliced
- 1 red onion, thinly sliced
- Cherry tomatoes, halved
- 2 tablespoons olive oil
- 1 teaspoon dried thyme
- Salt and black pepper to taste

For the Quinoa:

- 1 cup quinoa, rinsed
- 2 cups vegetable broth or water
- Salt to taste

For the Avocado-Lime Dressing:

- 1 ripe avocado, peeled and pitted
- Juice of 2 limes
- 2 tablespoons olive oil
- 2 cloves garlic, minced
- 1 tablespoon fresh cilantro, chopped
- Salt and black pepper to taste

Additional Ingredients:

- Mixed salad greens
- Avocado slices for garnish
- Toasted pumpkin seeds or nuts (optional)

Instructions:

Preheat the grill to medium-high heat.

In a bowl, toss zucchini, yellow squash, red bell pepper, red onion, and cherry tomatoes with olive oil, dried thyme, salt, and black pepper.

Grill the vegetables for about 8-10 minutes, turning occasionally, until they are tender and have a nice char.

While grilling, rinse quinoa under cold water. In a saucepan, combine quinoa and vegetable broth (or water). Bring to a boil, then reduce heat to low, cover, and simmer for 15-20 minutes or until quinoa is cooked and liquid is absorbed. Fluff with a fork and let it cool.

In a blender or food processor, combine peeled and pitted avocado, lime juice, olive oil, minced garlic, chopped cilantro, salt, and black pepper. Blend until smooth to create the avocado-lime dressing.

In a large bowl, assemble the quinoa bowl by combining grilled vegetables, cooked quinoa, and mixed salad greens.

Drizzle the avocado-lime dressing over the bowl.

Toss gently to combine all the ingredients.

Garnish with avocado slices and toasted pumpkin seeds or nuts if desired.

Serve the Grilled Vegetable Quinoa Bowl with Avocado-Lime Dressing at room temperature or chilled.

Enjoy this wholesome and flavorful quinoa bowl filled with grilled vegetables and a creamy avocado-lime dressing!

Grilled Chimichurri Flank Steak

Ingredients:

For the Chimichurri Sauce:

- 1 cup fresh parsley, chopped
- 1/2 cup fresh cilantro, chopped
- 4 cloves garlic, minced
- 1/4 cup red wine vinegar
- 1/2 cup extra virgin olive oil
- 1 teaspoon dried oregano
- 1/2 teaspoon red pepper flakes (adjust to taste)
- Salt and black pepper to taste

For the Flank Steak:

- 2 lbs flank steak
- Olive oil for brushing
- Salt and black pepper to taste

Instructions:

In a bowl, combine chopped fresh parsley, chopped fresh cilantro, minced garlic, red wine vinegar, extra virgin olive oil, dried oregano, red pepper flakes, salt, and black pepper. Mix well to create the chimichurri sauce. Set aside.

Preheat the grill to medium-high heat.

Brush the flank steak with olive oil and season with salt and black pepper.

Grill the flank steak for about 4-6 minutes per side, or until it reaches your desired level of doneness.

During the last minute of grilling, brush a generous amount of chimichurri sauce on both sides of the steak.

Remove the flank steak from the grill and let it rest for a few minutes.

Slice the flank steak against the grain into thin strips.

Serve the Grilled Chimichurri Flank Steak with additional chimichurri sauce on the side.

Enjoy this delicious and flavorful chimichurri-marinated grilled flank steak as a satisfying main course!

Grilled Mediterranean Veggie and Halloumi Skewers

Ingredients:

For the Marinade:

- 1/4 cup olive oil
- 2 tablespoons balsamic vinegar
- 2 cloves garlic, minced
- 1 teaspoon dried oregano
- 1 teaspoon dried thyme
- Salt and black pepper to taste

For the Skewers:

- Cherry tomatoes
- Zucchini, sliced
- Red bell pepper, cut into chunks
- Red onion, cut into wedges
- Halloumi cheese, cut into cubes
- Wooden skewers, soaked in water for 30 minutes

For Garnish:

- Fresh parsley, chopped
- Lemon wedges

Instructions:

In a bowl, whisk together olive oil, balsamic vinegar, minced garlic, dried oregano, dried thyme, salt, and black pepper to create the marinade.

Preheat the grill to medium-high heat.

Thread cherry tomatoes, zucchini slices, red bell pepper chunks, red onion wedges, and halloumi cheese cubes onto the soaked wooden skewers, alternating for a colorful mix.

Brush the skewers with the prepared marinade, ensuring they are well-coated.

Grill the skewers for about 8-10 minutes, turning occasionally, until the vegetables are tender and the halloumi has grill marks.

During grilling, baste the skewers with additional marinade for extra flavor.

Once the skewers are done, transfer them to a serving platter.

Garnish with chopped fresh parsley and lemon wedges.

Serve the Grilled Mediterranean Veggie and Halloumi Skewers hot, either as an appetizer or a side dish.

Enjoy these delightful and colorful Mediterranean veggie and halloumi skewers for a taste of freshness and Mediterranean flavors!

Grilled Honey Mustard Glazed Chicken Thighs

Ingredients:

For the Honey Mustard Glaze:

- 1/4 cup Dijon mustard
- 2 tablespoons honey
- 2 tablespoons soy sauce
- 1 tablespoon olive oil
- 1 teaspoon minced garlic
- Salt and black pepper to taste

For the Chicken Thighs:

- 8 bone-in, skin-on chicken thighs
- Olive oil for brushing
- Salt and black pepper to taste
- Fresh parsley, chopped (for garnish)

Instructions:

In a bowl, whisk together Dijon mustard, honey, soy sauce, olive oil, minced garlic, salt, and black pepper to create the honey mustard glaze.

Preheat the grill to medium-high heat.

Brush the chicken thighs with olive oil and season with salt and black pepper.

Place the chicken thighs on the grill and cook for about 6-8 minutes per side, or until the internal temperature reaches 165°F (74°C) and the chicken is cooked through with a nice char.

During the last few minutes of grilling, brush a generous amount of honey mustard glaze on both sides of the chicken thighs.

Remove the chicken thighs from the grill and let them rest for a few minutes.

Transfer the grilled chicken thighs to a serving platter.

Garnish with chopped fresh parsley.

Serve the Grilled Honey Mustard Glazed Chicken Thighs hot, accompanied by your favorite side dishes.

Enjoy these succulent and flavorful honey mustard glazed chicken thighs for a delicious and easy-to-make grilled dish!

Grilled Teriyaki Veggie and Tofu Skewers

Ingredients:

For the Teriyaki Marinade:

- 1/4 cup soy sauce
- 3 tablespoons honey
- 2 tablespoons mirin (sweet rice wine)
- 1 tablespoon rice vinegar
- 1 tablespoon sesame oil
- 2 cloves garlic, minced
- 1 teaspoon ginger, grated
- 1 tablespoon cornstarch (optional, for thickening)

For the Skewers:

- Extra-firm tofu, pressed and cut into cubes
- Cherry tomatoes
- Zucchini, sliced
- Bell peppers (assorted colors), cut into chunks
- Red onion, cut into wedges
- Wooden skewers, soaked in water for 30 minutes

For Garnish:

- Sesame seeds
- Green onions, sliced

Instructions:

In a bowl, whisk together soy sauce, honey, mirin, rice vinegar, sesame oil, minced garlic, grated ginger, and cornstarch (if using) to create the teriyaki marinade.

Press the tofu to remove excess water, then cut it into cubes.

Place the tofu cubes in a resealable plastic bag or a shallow dish. Pour half of the teriyaki marinade over the tofu, reserving the other half for basting. Marinate in the refrigerator for at least 30 minutes.

Preheat the grill to medium-high heat.

Thread the marinated tofu cubes, cherry tomatoes, zucchini slices, bell pepper chunks, and red onion wedges onto the soaked wooden skewers, alternating for a colorful mix.

Grill the skewers for about 10-12 minutes, turning occasionally, until the tofu is lightly browned and the vegetables are tender.

During grilling, baste the skewers with the reserved marinade for extra flavor.

Once the skewers are done, transfer them to a serving platter.

Garnish with sesame seeds and sliced green onions.

Serve the Grilled Teriyaki Veggie and Tofu Skewers hot, either as an appetizer or a main course.

Enjoy these tasty and satisfying teriyaki veggie and tofu skewers with a perfect balance of flavors!

Grilled Lemon Garlic Shrimp Skewers

Ingredients:

For the Marinade:

- 1/4 cup olive oil
- Zest and juice of 2 lemons
- 3 cloves garlic, minced
- 1 tablespoon fresh parsley, chopped
- 1 teaspoon dried oregano
- Salt and black pepper to taste

For the Shrimp Skewers:

- 1.5 lbs large shrimp, peeled and deveined
- Lemon slices (for garnish)
- Wooden skewers, soaked in water for 30 minutes

Instructions:

In a bowl, whisk together olive oil, lemon zest, lemon juice, minced garlic, chopped fresh parsley, dried oregano, salt, and black pepper to create the marinade.

Place the peeled and deveined shrimp in a resealable plastic bag or a shallow dish. Pour the marinade over the shrimp, ensuring they are well-coated. Marinate in the refrigerator for about 15-20 minutes.

Preheat the grill to medium-high heat.

Thread the marinated shrimp onto the soaked wooden skewers.

Grill the shrimp skewers for about 2-3 minutes per side, or until the shrimp are opaque and have a nice char.

During grilling, you can place lemon slices on the grill for a few seconds to get a light char.

Once the shrimp are done, transfer the skewers to a serving platter.

Garnish with grilled lemon slices.

Serve the Grilled Lemon Garlic Shrimp Skewers hot, either as an appetizer or a main course.

Enjoy these succulent and citrusy grilled lemon garlic shrimp skewers for a quick and delightful seafood dish!

Grilled Caprese Portobello Mushrooms

Ingredients:

For the Balsamic Glaze:

- 1/2 cup balsamic vinegar
- 2 tablespoons honey

For the Portobello Mushrooms:

- 4 large portobello mushroom caps, stems removed
- 3 tablespoons balsamic glaze (for marinating)
- 2 tablespoons olive oil
- 2 cloves garlic, minced
- Salt and black pepper to taste

For the Caprese Topping:

- Fresh mozzarella cheese, sliced
- Cherry tomatoes, sliced
- Fresh basil leaves
- Salt and black pepper to taste

Instructions:

In a small saucepan, combine balsamic vinegar and honey for the balsamic glaze. Bring to a simmer over medium heat, then reduce the heat to low. Simmer for about 10-15 minutes or until the glaze thickens. Remove from heat and let it cool.

Preheat the grill to medium-high heat.

Clean the portobello mushroom caps and remove the stems.

In a bowl, whisk together balsamic glaze, olive oil, minced garlic, salt, and black pepper.

Brush the mushroom caps with the prepared balsamic glaze mixture, ensuring they are well-coated.

Grill the mushroom caps for about 4-5 minutes per side, or until they are tender and have grill marks.

During grilling, add fresh mozzarella slices to the gill side of the mushrooms to melt slightly.

Once the mushrooms are done, transfer them to a serving platter.

Top each grilled mushroom cap with cherry tomato slices and fresh basil leaves.

Drizzle additional balsamic glaze over the top.

Season with salt and black pepper to taste.

Serve the Grilled Caprese Portobello Mushrooms hot, offering a flavorful and satisfying vegetarian dish.

Enjoy these delicious and visually appealing grilled caprese portobello mushrooms for a light and tasty meal!

Grilled Veggie and Hummus Wrap

Ingredients:

For the Marinade:

- 1/4 cup balsamic vinegar
- 2 tablespoons olive oil
- 2 cloves garlic, minced
- 1 teaspoon dried oregano
- Salt and black pepper to taste

For the Grilled Vegetables:

- Zucchini, sliced
- Yellow squash, sliced
- Red bell pepper, sliced
- Red onion, thinly sliced
- Cherry tomatoes

For the Wrap:

- Whole wheat or spinach tortillas
- Hummus (store-bought or homemade)
- Fresh spinach leaves
- Feta cheese, crumbled (optional)
- Kalamata olives, pitted and sliced
- Fresh parsley, chopped (for garnish)

Instructions:

In a bowl, whisk together balsamic vinegar, olive oil, minced garlic, dried oregano, salt, and black pepper to create the marinade.

Preheat the grill to medium-high heat.

Toss zucchini, yellow squash, red bell pepper, red onion, and cherry tomatoes in the marinade until well-coated.

Grill the vegetables for about 8-10 minutes, turning occasionally, until they are tender and have a nice char.

While grilling, warm the tortillas on the grill for about 10-15 seconds per side.

Spread a generous layer of hummus onto each tortilla.

Place a handful of fresh spinach leaves on top of the hummus.

Arrange a portion of the grilled vegetables on one side of the tortilla.

Optional: Sprinkle crumbled feta cheese over the vegetables.

Add sliced Kalamata olives and chopped fresh parsley for extra flavor.

Fold the tortilla, creating a wrap.

Repeat the process for additional wraps.

Serve the Grilled Veggie and Hummus Wraps warm, offering a tasty and nutritious meal.

Enjoy these grilled veggie and hummus wraps filled with Mediterranean-inspired flavors!

Grilled Pineapple Chicken Skewers with Teriyaki Glaze

Ingredients:

For the Teriyaki Marinade:

- 1/4 cup soy sauce
- 3 tablespoons honey
- 2 tablespoons rice vinegar
- 1 tablespoon sesame oil
- 2 cloves garlic, minced
- 1 teaspoon ginger, grated
- 1 tablespoon cornstarch (optional, for thickening)

For the Chicken Skewers:

- 1.5 lbs boneless, skinless chicken thighs, cut into cubes
- Fresh pineapple, cut into chunks
- Red bell pepper, cut into chunks
- Red onion, cut into wedges
- Wooden skewers, soaked in water for 30 minutes

For Garnish:

- Sesame seeds
- Green onions, sliced

Instructions:

In a bowl, whisk together soy sauce, honey, rice vinegar, sesame oil, minced garlic, grated ginger, and cornstarch (if using) to create the teriyaki marinade.

Place the chicken thigh cubes in a resealable plastic bag or a shallow dish. Pour half of the teriyaki marinade over the chicken, reserving the other half for basting. Marinate in the refrigerator for about 30 minutes.

Preheat the grill to medium-high heat.

Thread the marinated chicken cubes, pineapple chunks, red bell pepper chunks, and red onion wedges onto the soaked wooden skewers, alternating for a colorful mix.

Grill the skewers for about 10-12 minutes, turning occasionally, until the chicken is cooked through, and the pineapple and vegetables have a nice char.

During grilling, baste the skewers with the reserved marinade for extra flavor.

Once the skewers are done, transfer them to a serving platter.

Garnish with sesame seeds and sliced green onions.

Serve the Grilled Pineapple Chicken Skewers with Teriyaki Glaze hot, either as an appetizer or a main course.

Enjoy these delightful and savory grilled pineapple chicken skewers with a delicious teriyaki glaze!

Grilled Veggie Quesadillas with Avocado Salsa

Ingredients:

For the Grilled Vegetables:

- Zucchini, sliced
- Yellow squash, sliced
- Red bell pepper, sliced
- Red onion, thinly sliced
- 2 tablespoons olive oil
- 1 teaspoon ground cumin
- 1 teaspoon chili powder
- Salt and black pepper to taste

For the Avocado Salsa:

- 2 ripe avocados, diced
- 1 cup cherry tomatoes, halved
- 1/4 cup red onion, finely chopped
- 1/4 cup fresh cilantro, chopped
- Juice of 1 lime
- Salt and black pepper to taste

For the Quesadillas:

- Flour tortillas
- Shredded cheese (cheddar, Monterey Jack, or your choice)
- Sour cream (for serving)

Instructions:

Preheat the grill to medium-high heat.

In a bowl, toss zucchini, yellow squash, red bell pepper, red onion, olive oil, ground cumin, chili powder, salt, and black pepper until the vegetables are well-coated.

Grill the vegetables for about 8-10 minutes, turning occasionally, until they are tender and have a nice char.

While grilling, prepare the avocado salsa by combining diced avocados, cherry tomatoes, red onion, chopped cilantro, lime juice, salt, and black pepper. Mix gently and set aside.

On the grill, place flour tortillas and sprinkle shredded cheese on one half of each tortilla.

Once the cheese begins to melt, add a portion of the grilled vegetables on top of the cheese.

Fold the tortilla in half, creating a quesadilla.

Grill the quesadillas for about 2-3 minutes per side, or until they are golden brown and the cheese is melted.

Remove the quesadillas from the grill and let them rest for a minute.

Cut each quesadilla into wedges.

Serve the Grilled Veggie Quesadillas with Avocado Salsa hot, accompanied by sour cream.

Enjoy these flavorful and satisfying grilled veggie quesadillas with a refreshing avocado salsa!

Grilled Lemon Herb Salmon

Ingredients:

For the Lemon Herb Marinade:

- Juice of 2 lemons
- Zest of 1 lemon
- 3 tablespoons olive oil
- 2 cloves garlic, minced
- 1 tablespoon fresh parsley, chopped
- 1 teaspoon dried dill
- Salt and black pepper to taste

For the Salmon:

- 4 salmon fillets (about 6 ounces each)
- Lemon slices (for garnish)
- Fresh dill sprigs (for garnish)

Instructions:

In a bowl, whisk together lemon juice, lemon zest, olive oil, minced garlic, chopped fresh parsley, dried dill, salt, and black pepper to create the lemon herb marinade.

Place the salmon fillets in a shallow dish. Pour the lemon herb marinade over the salmon, ensuring they are well-coated. Marinate in the refrigerator for at least 30 minutes.

Preheat the grill to medium-high heat.

Remove the salmon fillets from the marinade and let excess marinade drip off.

Grill the salmon fillets for about 4-5 minutes per side, or until the salmon is cooked through and flakes easily with a fork.

During grilling, you can add lemon slices to the grill for a few seconds to get a light char.

Once the salmon is done, transfer it to a serving platter.

Garnish with grilled lemon slices and fresh dill sprigs.

Serve the Grilled Lemon Herb Salmon hot, accompanied by your favorite side dishes.

Enjoy this light and flavorful grilled lemon herb salmon for a healthy and delicious meal!

Grilled Peach and Goat Cheese Salad

Ingredients:

For the Grilled Peaches:

- 4 ripe peaches, halved and pitted
- 2 tablespoons honey
- 1 tablespoon olive oil

For the Salad:

- Mixed salad greens (arugula, spinach, or your choice)
- Goat cheese, crumbled
- Pecans or walnuts, toasted and chopped
- Balsamic glaze (store-bought or homemade)
- Salt and black pepper to taste

Instructions:

Preheat the grill to medium-high heat.

In a bowl, whisk together honey and olive oil.

Brush the cut side of each peach half with the honey and olive oil mixture.

Grill the peaches for about 2-3 minutes per side, or until they have grill marks and are slightly softened.

Remove the grilled peaches from the grill and let them cool for a few minutes.

Slice the grilled peaches into wedges.

In a large salad bowl, combine mixed salad greens, crumbled goat cheese, and toasted chopped nuts.

Add the sliced grilled peaches to the salad.

Drizzle balsamic glaze over the salad, and toss gently to combine all the ingredients.

Season with salt and black pepper to taste.

Serve the Grilled Peach and Goat Cheese Salad immediately, offering a sweet and savory combination.

Enjoy this refreshing and elegant grilled peach and goat cheese salad as a delightful appetizer or side dish!

Grilled Garlic-Lime Chicken Skewers

Ingredients:

For the Marinade:

- Juice of 3 limes
- Zest of 1 lime
- 3 tablespoons olive oil
- 4 cloves garlic, minced
- 1 teaspoon cumin
- 1 teaspoon smoked paprika
- 1 teaspoon dried oregano
- Salt and black pepper to taste

For the Chicken Skewers:

- 2 lbs boneless, skinless chicken breasts, cut into cubes
- Red onion, cut into wedges
- Cherry tomatoes
- Wooden skewers, soaked in water for 30 minutes

For Garnish:

- Fresh cilantro, chopped
- Lime wedges

Instructions:

In a bowl, whisk together lime juice, lime zest, olive oil, minced garlic, cumin, smoked paprika, dried oregano, salt, and black pepper to create the marinade.

Place the chicken cubes in a resealable plastic bag or a shallow dish. Pour the marinade over the chicken, ensuring it is well-coated. Marinate in the refrigerator for at least 30 minutes.

Preheat the grill to medium-high heat.

Thread the marinated chicken cubes, red onion wedges, and cherry tomatoes onto the soaked wooden skewers, alternating for a colorful mix.

Grill the skewers for about 8-10 minutes, turning occasionally, until the chicken is cooked through and has a nice char.

During grilling, you can baste the skewers with any remaining marinade for extra flavor.

Once the skewers are done, transfer them to a serving platter.

Garnish with chopped fresh cilantro and lime wedges.

Serve the Grilled Garlic-Lime Chicken Skewers hot, either as an appetizer or a main course.

Enjoy these zesty and flavorful grilled garlic-lime chicken skewers for a delicious and easy-to-make meal!

Grilled Portobello Mushroom Burgers with Basil Aioli

Ingredients:

For the Portobello Mushrooms:

- 4 large portobello mushroom caps
- 3 tablespoons balsamic vinegar
- 2 tablespoons olive oil
- 2 cloves garlic, minced
- Salt and black pepper to taste

For the Basil Aioli:

- 1 cup mayonnaise
- 1/4 cup fresh basil leaves, chopped
- 1 clove garlic, minced
- Juice of 1 lemon
- Salt and black pepper to taste

For the Burger Assembly:

- Whole wheat burger buns
- Mixed salad greens
- Tomato slices
- Red onion rings

Instructions:

Preheat the grill to medium-high heat.

Clean the portobello mushroom caps and remove the stems.

In a bowl, whisk together balsamic vinegar, olive oil, minced garlic, salt, and black pepper.

Brush both sides of the portobello mushroom caps with the balsamic marinade.

Grill the mushrooms for about 4-5 minutes per side, or until they are tender and have grill marks.

While grilling, prepare the basil aioli by combining mayonnaise, chopped fresh basil, minced garlic, lemon juice, salt, and black pepper. Mix well.

Toast the whole wheat burger buns on the grill for a minute or two.

Assemble the burgers by spreading a generous layer of basil aioli on the bottom half of each bun.

Place a grilled portobello mushroom cap on top of the aioli.

Add mixed salad greens, tomato slices, and red onion rings.

Top with the other half of the bun.

Serve the Grilled Portobello Mushroom Burgers with Basil Aioli immediately, offering a savory and satisfying vegetarian option.

Enjoy these delicious and hearty grilled portobello mushroom burgers with a flavorful basil aioli!

Grilled Teriyaki Pineapple Turkey Burgers

Ingredients:

For the Teriyaki Pineapple Glaze:

- 1/2 cup soy sauce
- 1/4 cup pineapple juice
- 2 tablespoons honey
- 1 tablespoon rice vinegar
- 1 teaspoon sesame oil
- 1 teaspoon ginger, grated
- 2 cloves garlic, minced
- 1 tablespoon cornstarch (optional, for thickening)

For the Turkey Burgers:

- 1.5 lbs ground turkey
- 1/2 cup breadcrumbs
- 1/4 cup green onions, finely chopped
- 1 teaspoon garlic powder
- Salt and black pepper to taste
- Burger buns

For Garnish:

- Grilled pineapple slices
- Lettuce leaves
- Red onion, thinly sliced

Instructions:

In a small saucepan, whisk together soy sauce, pineapple juice, honey, rice vinegar, sesame oil, grated ginger, minced garlic, and cornstarch (if using) to create the teriyaki pineapple glaze. Bring to a simmer over medium heat, stirring constantly until it thickens. Remove from heat and let it cool.

Preheat the grill to medium-high heat.

In a bowl, combine ground turkey, breadcrumbs, chopped green onions, garlic powder, salt, and black pepper. Mix until well combined.

Shape the turkey mixture into burger patties.

Grill the turkey burgers for about 5-6 minutes per side, or until they are cooked through and have grill marks.

During grilling, brush the burgers with the teriyaki pineapple glaze for extra flavor.

In the last minute of grilling, place pineapple slices on the grill and cook for about 30 seconds per side.

Toast the burger buns on the grill for a minute.

Assemble the burgers by placing a turkey patty on the bottom half of each bun.

Top with grilled pineapple slices, lettuce leaves, and thinly sliced red onion.

Drizzle additional teriyaki pineapple glaze on top.

Add the other half of the bun.

Serve the Grilled Teriyaki Pineapple Turkey Burgers hot, offering a sweet and savory twist to classic turkey burgers.

Enjoy these delicious and flavorful grilled teriyaki pineapple turkey burgers for a tasty and unique burger experience!

Grilled Teriyaki Salmon Bowls

Ingredients:

For the Teriyaki Marinade:

- 1/2 cup soy sauce
- 1/4 cup mirin (sweet rice wine)
- 2 tablespoons honey
- 1 tablespoon rice vinegar
- 1 teaspoon sesame oil
- 2 cloves garlic, minced
- 1 teaspoon ginger, grated
- 1 tablespoon cornstarch (optional, for thickening)

For the Salmon:

- 4 salmon fillets
- Salt and black pepper to taste
- Sesame seeds (for garnish)

For the Grilled Vegetables:

- Broccoli florets
- Carrots, sliced
- Bell peppers (assorted colors), sliced
- Zucchini, sliced
- 2 tablespoons olive oil
- Salt and black pepper to taste

For the Bowls:

- Cooked brown rice or quinoa
- Avocado slices
- Green onions, sliced
- Sesame seeds (for garnish)

Instructions:

In a bowl, whisk together soy sauce, mirin, honey, rice vinegar, sesame oil, minced garlic, grated ginger, and cornstarch (if using) to create the teriyaki marinade.

Preheat the grill to medium-high heat.

Season the salmon fillets with salt and black pepper.

Brush the salmon fillets with the teriyaki marinade.

Grill the salmon for about 4-5 minutes per side, or until it flakes easily with a fork and has grill marks. Sprinkle sesame seeds on top.

In a bowl, toss broccoli florets, sliced carrots, bell peppers, and zucchini with olive oil, salt, and black pepper.

Grill the vegetables for about 8-10 minutes, turning occasionally, until they are tender and have a nice char.

While grilling, cook brown rice or quinoa according to package instructions.

Assemble the bowls by placing a serving of brown rice or quinoa in each bowl.

Top with grilled teriyaki salmon, grilled vegetables, avocado slices, and sliced green onions.

Garnish with sesame seeds.

Drizzle additional teriyaki marinade over the bowls if desired.

Serve the Grilled Teriyaki Salmon Bowls hot, offering a flavorful and wholesome meal.

Enjoy these delicious and nutritious grilled teriyaki salmon bowls for a satisfying and well-balanced dinner!

Grilled Herb-Marinated Lamb Chops

Ingredients:

For the Herb Marinade:

- 1/4 cup olive oil
- 2 tablespoons fresh rosemary, chopped
- 2 tablespoons fresh thyme, chopped
- 3 cloves garlic, minced
- Zest and juice of 1 lemon
- Salt and black pepper to taste

For the Lamb Chops:

- 8 lamb chops (about 1 inch thick)
- Salt and black pepper to taste

For Garnish:

- Fresh mint leaves, chopped
- Lemon wedges

Instructions:

In a bowl, whisk together olive oil, chopped fresh rosemary, chopped fresh thyme, minced garlic, lemon zest, lemon juice, salt, and black pepper to create the herb marinade.

Season the lamb chops with salt and black pepper.

Place the lamb chops in a shallow dish and pour the herb marinade over them. Ensure the chops are well-coated. Marinate in the refrigerator for at least 30 minutes.

Preheat the grill to medium-high heat.

Grill the lamb chops for about 4-5 minutes per side, or until they reach your desired level of doneness and have a nice char.

During grilling, baste the lamb chops with the remaining herb marinade for extra flavor.

Once the lamb chops are done, transfer them to a serving platter.

Garnish with chopped fresh mint leaves and lemon wedges.

Serve the Grilled Herb-Marinated Lamb Chops hot, offering a flavorful and elegant dish.

Enjoy these succulent and herb-marinated lamb chops for a delightful and impressive grilling experience!

Grilled Sweet Potato and Black Bean Quesadillas

Ingredients:

For the Sweet Potato Filling:

- 2 medium sweet potatoes, peeled and diced
- 1 tablespoon olive oil
- 1 teaspoon ground cumin
- 1 teaspoon chili powder
- Salt and black pepper to taste

For the Black Bean and Corn Salsa:

- 1 can (15 oz) black beans, drained and rinsed
- 1 cup corn kernels (fresh or frozen)
- 1/4 cup red onion, finely chopped
- 1/4 cup fresh cilantro, chopped
- Juice of 1 lime
- Salt and black pepper to taste

For the Quesadillas:

- Flour tortillas
- Shredded cheese (cheddar, Monterey Jack, or your choice)
- Avocado slices (for serving)
- Sour cream (for serving)

Instructions:

Preheat the grill to medium-high heat.

Toss diced sweet potatoes with olive oil, ground cumin, chili powder, salt, and black pepper.

Grill the sweet potatoes for about 8-10 minutes, turning occasionally, until they are tender and have grill marks.

In a bowl, combine black beans, corn kernels, chopped red onion, chopped cilantro, lime juice, salt, and black pepper to create the salsa. Mix well.

On the grill, place flour tortillas and sprinkle shredded cheese on one half of each tortilla. Once the cheese begins to melt, add a portion of grilled sweet potatoes and a generous spoonful of the black bean and corn salsa on top.

Fold the tortilla in half, creating a quesadilla.

Grill the quesadillas for about 2-3 minutes per side, or until they are golden brown and the cheese is melted.

Remove the quesadillas from the grill and let them rest for a minute.

Cut each quesadilla into wedges.

Serve the Grilled Sweet Potato and Black Bean Quesadillas warm, accompanied by avocado slices and sour cream.

Enjoy these delicious and satisfying grilled sweet potato and black bean quesadillas for a flavorful vegetarian meal!

Grilled Mediterranean Chicken Salad

Ingredients:

For the Grilled Chicken:

- 4 boneless, skinless chicken breasts
- 2 tablespoons olive oil
- 2 cloves garlic, minced
- 1 teaspoon dried oregano
- 1 teaspoon dried thyme
- Juice of 1 lemon
- Salt and black pepper to taste

For the Salad:

- Mixed salad greens (lettuce, spinach, arugula)
- Cherry tomatoes, halved
- Cucumber, sliced
- Red bell pepper, sliced
- Kalamata olives, pitted
- Red onion, thinly sliced
- Feta cheese, crumbled

For the Greek Dressing:

- 1/4 cup extra virgin olive oil
- 2 tablespoons red wine vinegar
- 1 teaspoon Dijon mustard

- 1 teaspoon dried oregano
- Salt and black pepper to taste

Instructions:

Preheat the grill to medium-high heat.

In a bowl, whisk together olive oil, minced garlic, dried oregano, dried thyme, lemon juice, salt, and black pepper to create the marinade for the chicken.

Brush the chicken breasts with the marinade, ensuring they are well-coated.

Grill the chicken breasts for about 6-7 minutes per side, or until they are cooked through and have grill marks.

In a separate bowl, whisk together extra virgin olive oil, red wine vinegar, Dijon mustard, dried oregano, salt, and black pepper to create the Greek dressing.

In a large salad bowl, combine mixed salad greens, cherry tomatoes, cucumber slices, red bell pepper slices, Kalamata olives, red onion slices, and crumbled feta cheese.

Slice the grilled chicken breasts and arrange them on top of the salad.

Drizzle the Greek dressing over the salad.

Toss the salad gently to combine all the ingredients.

Serve the Grilled Mediterranean Chicken Salad immediately, offering a fresh and flavorful dish.

Enjoy this vibrant and wholesome grilled Mediterranean chicken salad for a light and satisfying meal!

Grilled Shrimp Tacos with Avocado Lime Crema

Ingredients:

For the Grilled Shrimp:

- 1 lb large shrimp, peeled and deveined
- 2 tablespoons olive oil
- 2 cloves garlic, minced
- 1 teaspoon smoked paprika
- 1 teaspoon cumin
- Salt and black pepper to taste
- Wooden skewers, soaked in water for 30 minutes

For the Avocado Lime Crema:

- 1 ripe avocado
- 1/2 cup Greek yogurt
- Juice of 2 limes
- 2 tablespoons fresh cilantro, chopped
- Salt and black pepper to taste

For the Tacos:

- Corn or flour tortillas
- Shredded cabbage or lettuce
- Cherry tomatoes, halved
- Red onion, thinly sliced
- Fresh cilantro, chopped (for garnish)

- Lime wedges

Instructions:

Preheat the grill to medium-high heat.

In a bowl, combine olive oil, minced garlic, smoked paprika, cumin, salt, and black pepper for the shrimp marinade.

Toss the shrimp in the marinade until well-coated.

Thread the marinated shrimp onto soaked wooden skewers.

Grill the shrimp skewers for about 2-3 minutes per side, or until the shrimp are opaque and have grill marks.

In a blender or food processor, combine ripe avocado, Greek yogurt, lime juice, chopped cilantro, salt, and black pepper. Blend until smooth to create the avocado lime crema.

Warm the tortillas on the grill for about 10-15 seconds per side.

Assemble the tacos by spreading a spoonful of avocado lime crema on each tortilla.

Place shredded cabbage or lettuce on top of the crema.

Add grilled shrimp from the skewers.

Top with cherry tomatoes, thinly sliced red onion, and chopped fresh cilantro.

Squeeze lime wedges over the tacos for extra freshness.

Serve the Grilled Shrimp Tacos with Avocado Lime Crema hot, offering a zesty and satisfying taco experience.

Enjoy these delicious and flavorful grilled shrimp tacos with creamy avocado lime crema!

Grilled Vegetable and Halloumi Skewers with Lemon Herb Marinade

Ingredients:

For the Lemon Herb Marinade:

- 1/4 cup olive oil
- Zest and juice of 1 lemon
- 2 cloves garlic, minced
- 1 tablespoon fresh rosemary, chopped
- 1 tablespoon fresh thyme, chopped
- Salt and black pepper to taste

For the Skewers:

- Cherry tomatoes
- Zucchini, sliced
- Yellow squash, sliced
- Red bell pepper, cut into chunks
- Red onion, cut into wedges
- Halloumi cheese, cut into cubes

For Garnish:

- Fresh parsley, chopped
- Lemon wedges

Instructions:

  Preheat the grill to medium-high heat.

In a bowl, whisk together olive oil, lemon zest, lemon juice, minced garlic, chopped rosemary, chopped thyme, salt, and black pepper to create the lemon herb marinade.

Toss cherry tomatoes, sliced zucchini, sliced yellow squash, red bell pepper chunks, red onion wedges, and halloumi cubes in the marinade until well-coated.

Thread the marinated vegetables and halloumi onto skewers, alternating for a colorful mix.

Grill the skewers for about 8-10 minutes, turning occasionally, until the vegetables are tender and halloumi has a nice golden color.

While grilling, baste the skewers with any remaining marinade for extra flavor.

Once the skewers are done, transfer them to a serving platter.

Garnish with chopped fresh parsley and lemon wedges.

Serve the Grilled Vegetable and Halloumi Skewers hot, offering a delightful and flavorful dish.

Enjoy these tasty and colorful grilled vegetable and halloumi skewers with a zesty lemon herb marinade!

Grilled Lemon Garlic Shrimp Pasta

Ingredients:

For the Grilled Lemon Garlic Shrimp:

- 1 lb large shrimp, peeled and deveined
- 3 tablespoons olive oil
- Zest and juice of 2 lemons
- 4 cloves garlic, minced
- 1 teaspoon dried oregano
- Salt and black pepper to taste
- Wooden skewers, soaked in water for 30 minutes

For the Pasta:

- 12 oz linguine or your favorite pasta
- 2 tablespoons olive oil
- Cherry tomatoes, halved
- Baby spinach leaves
- Fresh basil, chopped
- Grated Parmesan cheese (for serving)

Instructions:

Preheat the grill to medium-high heat.

In a bowl, combine olive oil, lemon zest, lemon juice, minced garlic, dried oregano, salt, and black pepper for the shrimp marinade.

Toss the shrimp in the marinade until well-coated.

Thread the marinated shrimp onto soaked wooden skewers.

Grill the shrimp skewers for about 2-3 minutes per side, or until the shrimp are opaque and have grill marks.

In the meantime, cook the pasta according to package instructions.

In a large pan, heat olive oil over medium heat. Add halved cherry tomatoes and sauté for 2-3 minutes until they start to soften.

Add baby spinach leaves to the pan and cook until wilted.

Toss the cooked and drained pasta into the pan with the vegetables, mixing well.

Remove the shrimp from the skewers and add them to the pasta.

Sprinkle chopped fresh basil over the pasta and toss to combine.

Serve the Grilled Lemon Garlic Shrimp Pasta hot, garnished with grated Parmesan cheese.

Enjoy this light and flavorful grilled lemon garlic shrimp pasta for a delightful and easy-to-make meal!

Grilled Honey Mustard Chicken Skewers

Ingredients:

For the Honey Mustard Marinade:

- 1/4 cup Dijon mustard
- 2 tablespoons honey
- 2 tablespoons olive oil
- 1 tablespoon apple cider vinegar
- 2 cloves garlic, minced
- Salt and black pepper to taste

For the Chicken Skewers:

- 1.5 lbs boneless, skinless chicken breasts, cut into cubes
- Wooden skewers, soaked in water for 30 minutes

For Garnish:

- Fresh parsley, chopped
- Lemon wedges

Instructions:

In a bowl, whisk together Dijon mustard, honey, olive oil, apple cider vinegar, minced garlic, salt, and black pepper to create the honey mustard marinade.

Place the chicken cubes in a shallow dish and pour the marinade over them. Ensure the chicken is well-coated. Marinate in the refrigerator for at least 30 minutes.

Preheat the grill to medium-high heat.

Thread the marinated chicken cubes onto soaked wooden skewers.

Grill the chicken skewers for about 6-8 minutes, turning occasionally, until the chicken is cooked through and has a nice char.

During grilling, baste the skewers with any remaining marinade for extra flavor.

Once the skewers are done, transfer them to a serving platter.

Garnish with chopped fresh parsley and lemon wedges.

Serve the Grilled Honey Mustard Chicken Skewers hot, offering a sweet and tangy twist to classic grilled chicken.

Enjoy these delicious and succulent grilled honey mustard chicken skewers for a flavorful and satisfying meal!

Grilled Veggie and Hummus Wraps

Ingredients:

For the Grilled Vegetables:

- Zucchini, sliced
- Yellow squash, sliced
- Red bell pepper, cut into strips
- Red onion, sliced
- Cherry tomatoes, halved
- 2 tablespoons olive oil
- 1 teaspoon dried Italian herbs
- Salt and black pepper to taste

For the Hummus Spread:

- 1 cup hummus (store-bought or homemade)
- Juice of 1 lemon
- 1 clove garlic, minced
- Salt and black pepper to taste

For the Wraps:

- Whole wheat or spinach wraps
- Fresh spinach leaves
- Avocado slices
- Feta cheese, crumbled
- Fresh basil or cilantro, chopped

Instructions:

Preheat the grill to medium-high heat.

In a bowl, toss zucchini, yellow squash, red bell pepper, red onion, and cherry tomatoes with olive oil, dried Italian herbs, salt, and black pepper.

Grill the vegetables for about 8-10 minutes, turning occasionally, until they are tender and have a nice char.

In a separate bowl, mix hummus, lemon juice, minced garlic, salt, and black pepper to create the hummus spread.

Warm the wraps on the grill for about 10 seconds per side.

Spread a generous layer of hummus spread on each wrap.

Add a handful of fresh spinach leaves on top of the hummus.

Arrange grilled vegetables on the wraps.

Add avocado slices, crumbled feta cheese, and chopped fresh basil or cilantro.

Fold the sides of the wraps and roll them up tightly.

Slice the wraps in half diagonally.

Serve the Grilled Veggie and Hummus Wraps immediately, offering a delicious and nutritious wrap option.

Enjoy these flavorful and wholesome grilled veggie and hummus wraps for a satisfying and healthy meal!

Grilled Pineapple Chicken Skewers with Teriyaki Glaze

Ingredients:

For the Teriyaki Glaze:

- 1/2 cup soy sauce
- 1/4 cup pineapple juice
- 2 tablespoons honey
- 1 tablespoon rice vinegar
- 1 teaspoon sesame oil
- 1 teaspoon ginger, grated
- 2 cloves garlic, minced
- 1 tablespoon cornstarch (optional, for thickening)

For the Chicken Skewers:

- 1.5 lbs boneless, skinless chicken thighs, cut into cubes
- Fresh pineapple chunks
- Red bell pepper, cut into chunks
- Red onion, cut into wedges
- Wooden skewers, soaked in water for 30 minutes

For Garnish:

- Green onions, sliced
- Sesame seeds
- Chopped cilantro

Instructions:

In a small saucepan, whisk together soy sauce, pineapple juice, honey, rice vinegar, sesame oil, grated ginger, minced garlic, and cornstarch (if using) to create the teriyaki glaze. Bring to a simmer over medium heat, stirring constantly until it thickens. Remove from heat and let it cool.

Preheat the grill to medium-high heat.

Thread the chicken cubes, fresh pineapple chunks, red bell pepper chunks, and red onion wedges onto soaked wooden skewers, alternating for a colorful mix.

Grill the skewers for about 8-10 minutes, turning occasionally, until the chicken is cooked through and has a nice char.

During grilling, baste the skewers with the teriyaki glaze for extra flavor.

Once the skewers are done, transfer them to a serving platter.

Garnish with sliced green onions, sesame seeds, and chopped cilantro.

Serve the Grilled Pineapple Chicken Skewers with Teriyaki Glaze hot, offering a sweet and savory tropical delight.

Enjoy these delicious and vibrant grilled pineapple chicken skewers with a flavorful teriyaki glaze!

Grilled Tofu and Vegetable Kebabs with Peanut Sauce

Ingredients:

For the Tofu Marinade:

- 14 oz extra-firm tofu, pressed and cut into cubes
- 3 tablespoons soy sauce
- 1 tablespoon sesame oil
- 1 tablespoon maple syrup or agave nectar
- 1 teaspoon garlic powder
- 1 teaspoon ginger, grated

For the Vegetable Kebabs:

- Cherry tomatoes
- Bell peppers (assorted colors), cut into chunks
- Red onion, cut into wedges
- Zucchini, sliced
- Wooden skewers, soaked in water for 30 minutes

For the Peanut Sauce:

- 1/4 cup peanut butter
- 2 tablespoons soy sauce
- 1 tablespoon rice vinegar
- 1 tablespoon maple syrup or agave nectar
- 1 teaspoon sesame oil
- 1 clove garlic, minced

- Water (to adjust consistency)

For Garnish:

- Fresh cilantro, chopped
- Crushed peanuts

Instructions:

In a bowl, whisk together soy sauce, sesame oil, maple syrup (or agave nectar), garlic powder, and grated ginger for the tofu marinade.

Place the tofu cubes in a shallow dish and pour the marinade over them. Ensure the tofu is well-coated. Marinate for at least 30 minutes.

Preheat the grill to medium-high heat.

Thread the marinated tofu cubes, cherry tomatoes, bell pepper chunks, red onion wedges, and zucchini slices onto soaked wooden skewers.

Grill the kebabs for about 8-10 minutes, turning occasionally, until the tofu is golden and the vegetables are tender.

In a bowl, whisk together peanut butter, soy sauce, rice vinegar, maple syrup (or agave nectar), sesame oil, and minced garlic to create the peanut sauce. Adjust the consistency with water if needed.

Once the kebabs are done, transfer them to a serving platter.

Drizzle the peanut sauce over the kebabs.

Garnish with chopped fresh cilantro and crushed peanuts.

Serve the Grilled Tofu and Vegetable Kebabs with Peanut Sauce hot, offering a flavorful and protein-packed dish.

Enjoy these tasty and satisfying grilled tofu and vegetable kebabs with a delicious peanut sauce!

Grilled Eggplant and Mozzarella Panini

Ingredients:

For the Grilled Eggplant:

- 1 large eggplant, sliced into rounds
- 3 tablespoons olive oil
- 2 cloves garlic, minced
- 1 teaspoon dried oregano
- Salt and black pepper to taste

For the Panini:

- Ciabatta bread or your favorite sandwich bread
- Fresh mozzarella, sliced
- Fresh basil leaves
- Sun-dried tomatoes, drained and sliced
- Balsamic glaze (optional)

Instructions:

Preheat the grill to medium-high heat.

In a bowl, whisk together olive oil, minced garlic, dried oregano, salt, and black pepper.

Brush both sides of the eggplant slices with the olive oil mixture.

Grill the eggplant slices for about 3-4 minutes per side, or until they are tender and have grill marks.

While grilling, slice the ciabatta bread and assemble the panini with fresh mozzarella, grilled eggplant slices, fresh basil leaves, and sun-dried tomatoes.

Once the eggplant slices are done, remove them from the grill.

Preheat a panini press or grill pan.

Place the assembled panini on the panini press or grill pan and cook until the bread is golden and the cheese is melted.

If using a panini press, follow the manufacturer's instructions for pressing.

Drizzle with balsamic glaze if desired.

Remove the panini from the press or grill pan.

Serve the Grilled Eggplant and Mozzarella Panini hot, offering a delicious and flavorful sandwich.

Enjoy this grilled eggplant and mozzarella panini as a tasty and satisfying meal!

Grilled Lemon Herb Salmon with Asparagus

Ingredients:

For the Lemon Herb Marinade:

- 1/4 cup olive oil
- Zest and juice of 2 lemons
- 2 cloves garlic, minced
- 1 tablespoon fresh dill, chopped
- 1 tablespoon fresh parsley, chopped
- Salt and black pepper to taste

For the Salmon and Asparagus:

- 4 salmon fillets
- Fresh asparagus spears, trimmed
- Lemon slices (for garnish)

Instructions:

In a bowl, whisk together olive oil, lemon zest, lemon juice, minced garlic, chopped fresh dill, chopped fresh parsley, salt, and black pepper to create the lemon herb marinade. Place the salmon fillets in a shallow dish and pour the marinade over them. Ensure the salmon is well-coated. Marinate for at least 30 minutes.
Preheat the grill to medium-high heat.
Toss trimmed asparagus spears with a drizzle of olive oil, salt, and black pepper.
Grill the salmon fillets for about 4-5 minutes per side, or until they are cooked through and have grill marks. Place lemon slices on top of each fillet.

During grilling, add the asparagus spears to the grill and cook for about 3-4 minutes, turning occasionally, until they are tender-crisp.

Remove the salmon and asparagus from the grill.

Serve the Grilled Lemon Herb Salmon with Asparagus hot, garnished with additional lemon slices.

Enjoy this light and flavorful grilled lemon herb salmon with perfectly grilled asparagus for a delightful and nutritious meal!

Grilled Portobello Mushroom Burgers with Balsamic Glaze

Ingredients:

For the Portobello Marinade:

- 4 large portobello mushroom caps, stems removed
- 1/4 cup balsamic vinegar
- 3 tablespoons olive oil
- 2 cloves garlic, minced
- 1 teaspoon dried thyme
- Salt and black pepper to taste

For the Balsamic Glaze:

- 1/2 cup balsamic vinegar
- 2 tablespoons honey or maple syrup

For the Burger Assembly:

- Whole wheat burger buns
- Fresh spinach or arugula leaves
- Sliced tomatoes
- Red onion, thinly sliced
- Goat cheese or feta (optional)
- Dijon mustard or your favorite burger condiments

Instructions:

In a bowl, whisk together balsamic vinegar, olive oil, minced garlic, dried thyme, salt, and black pepper to create the portobello marinade.

Brush the portobello mushroom caps with the marinade, ensuring they are well-coated. Marinate for at least 30 minutes.

Preheat the grill to medium-high heat.

In a small saucepan, combine balsamic vinegar and honey (or maple syrup) for the balsamic glaze. Bring to a simmer over medium heat and cook until the mixture thickens slightly. Remove from heat and let it cool.

Grill the marinated portobello mushroom caps for about 4-5 minutes per side, or until they are tender and have grill marks.

While grilling, toast the whole wheat burger buns on the grill for about 1-2 minutes.

Assemble the burgers by placing a grilled portobello mushroom cap on the bottom half of each bun.

Top with fresh spinach or arugula leaves, sliced tomatoes, thinly sliced red onion, and goat cheese or feta if desired.

Drizzle the balsamic glaze over the toppings.

Spread Dijon mustard or your favorite burger condiments on the top half of the bun.

Place the top bun on the assembled ingredients to complete the burger.

Serve the Grilled Portobello Mushroom Burgers with Balsamic Glaze hot, offering a savory and satisfying vegetarian burger option.

Enjoy these delicious and hearty grilled portobello mushroom burgers with a flavorful balsamic glaze!

Grilled Vegetable and Quinoa Stuffed Peppers

Ingredients:

For the Quinoa:

- 1 cup quinoa, rinsed
- 2 cups vegetable broth or water
- 1 teaspoon olive oil
- Salt to taste

For the Grilled Vegetables:

- Zucchini, diced
- Red bell pepper, diced
- Yellow bell pepper, diced
- Red onion, diced
- Cherry tomatoes, halved
- 2 tablespoons olive oil
- 1 teaspoon dried Italian herbs
- Salt and black pepper to taste

For the Stuffed Peppers:

- Bell peppers (assorted colors), halved and seeds removed
- 1 cup feta cheese, crumbled
- Fresh parsley, chopped (for garnish)
- Lemon wedges (for serving)

Instructions:

Rinse quinoa under cold water. In a saucepan, combine quinoa, vegetable broth (or water), olive oil, and a pinch of salt. Bring to a boil, then reduce heat, cover, and simmer until quinoa is cooked and liquid is absorbed. Fluff with a fork and set aside.

Preheat the grill to medium-high heat.

In a bowl, toss diced zucchini, diced red and yellow bell pepper, diced red onion, and halved cherry tomatoes with olive oil, dried Italian herbs, salt, and black pepper.

Grill the vegetables for about 8-10 minutes, turning occasionally, until they are tender and have a nice char.

While grilling, halve bell peppers and remove seeds.

In a large bowl, mix grilled vegetables with cooked quinoa and crumbled feta cheese.

Stuff each bell pepper half with the quinoa and vegetable mixture.

Place the stuffed peppers on the grill for an additional 5-7 minutes, or until they are heated through.

Remove the stuffed peppers from the grill and garnish with chopped fresh parsley.

Serve the Grilled Vegetable and Quinoa Stuffed Peppers hot, accompanied by lemon wedges.

Enjoy these flavorful and nutritious grilled vegetable and quinoa stuffed peppers as a wholesome meal!

Grilled Teriyaki Tofu Skewers with Pineapple

Ingredients:

For the Teriyaki Marinade:

- 1/2 cup soy sauce
- 1/4 cup water
- 2 tablespoons maple syrup or agave nectar
- 1 tablespoon rice vinegar
- 1 teaspoon sesame oil
- 2 cloves garlic, minced
- 1 teaspoon ginger, grated
- 1 tablespoon cornstarch (optional, for thickening)

For the Tofu Skewers:

- 14 oz extra-firm tofu, pressed and cut into cubes
- Fresh pineapple chunks
- Red bell pepper, cut into chunks
- Red onion, cut into wedges
- Wooden skewers, soaked in water for 30 minutes

For Garnish:

- Sesame seeds
- Green onions, sliced
- Cooked white or brown rice

Instructions:

In a bowl, whisk together soy sauce, water, maple syrup (or agave nectar), rice vinegar, sesame oil, minced garlic, grated ginger, and cornstarch (if using) to create the teriyaki marinade.

Cut pressed tofu into cubes and place them in a shallow dish. Pour the teriyaki marinade over the tofu, ensuring it is well-coated. Marinate for at least 30 minutes.

Preheat the grill to medium-high heat.

Thread marinated tofu cubes, fresh pineapple chunks, red bell pepper chunks, and red onion wedges onto soaked wooden skewers, alternating for a colorful mix.

Grill the skewers for about 8-10 minutes, turning occasionally, until the tofu is golden and the vegetables are tender.

While grilling, baste the skewers with any remaining teriyaki marinade for extra flavor.

Once the skewers are done, transfer them to a serving platter.

Garnish with sesame seeds and sliced green onions.

Serve the Grilled Teriyaki Tofu Skewers with Pineapple over cooked white or brown rice for a complete and satisfying meal.

Enjoy these delicious and flavorful grilled teriyaki tofu skewers with a tropical twist!

Grilled Caprese Stuffed Portobello Mushrooms

Ingredients:

For the Balsamic Glaze:

- 1/2 cup balsamic vinegar
- 2 tablespoons honey or maple syrup

For the Portobello Mushrooms:

- 4 large portobello mushroom caps, stems removed
- 2 tablespoons olive oil
- 2 cloves garlic, minced
- Salt and black pepper to taste

For the Caprese Filling:

- Fresh mozzarella cheese, sliced
- Tomatoes, sliced
- Fresh basil leaves
- Balsamic glaze (from above)

Instructions:

In a small saucepan, combine balsamic vinegar and honey (or maple syrup) for the balsamic glaze. Bring to a simmer over medium heat and cook until the mixture thickens slightly. Remove from heat and let it cool.

Preheat the grill to medium-high heat.

Clean portobello mushroom caps and remove the stems.

In a bowl, whisk together olive oil, minced garlic, salt, and black pepper.

Brush both sides of the portobello mushroom caps with the olive oil mixture.

Grill the portobello mushrooms for about 4-5 minutes per side, or until they are tender and have grill marks.

While grilling, assemble the caprese filling by layering fresh mozzarella slices, tomato slices, and fresh basil leaves.

Once the portobello mushrooms are done, place them on a serving platter.

Fill each mushroom cap with the caprese filling.

Drizzle the balsamic glaze over the caprese-stuffed portobello mushrooms.

Serve the Grilled Caprese Stuffed Portobello Mushrooms hot, offering a flavorful and elegant appetizer or side dish.

Enjoy these delicious and visually appealing grilled caprese stuffed portobello mushrooms for a delightful dining experience!

Grilled Lemon Herb Chicken with Mediterranean Couscous Salad

Ingredients:

For the Grilled Lemon Herb Chicken:

- 4 boneless, skinless chicken breasts
- 3 tablespoons olive oil
- Zest and juice of 2 lemons
- 2 cloves garlic, minced
- 1 teaspoon dried oregano
- 1 teaspoon dried thyme
- Salt and black pepper to taste

For the Mediterranean Couscous Salad:

- 1 cup couscous
- 1.5 cups vegetable broth or water
- 2 tablespoons olive oil
- Cherry tomatoes, halved
- Cucumber, diced
- Kalamata olives, pitted and sliced
- Red onion, finely chopped
- Feta cheese, crumbled
- Fresh parsley, chopped
- Salt and black pepper to taste

Instructions:

For the Grilled Lemon Herb Chicken:

- In a bowl, whisk together olive oil, lemon zest, lemon juice, minced garlic, dried oregano, dried thyme, salt, and black pepper to create the marinade.
- Place the chicken breasts in a shallow dish and pour the marinade over them. Ensure the chicken is well-coated. Marinate for at least 30 minutes.
- Preheat the grill to medium-high heat.
- Grill the chicken breasts for about 6-7 minutes per side, or until they are cooked through and have grill marks.
- Remove the grilled chicken from the grill and let it rest for a few minutes before slicing.

For the Mediterranean Couscous Salad:

- In a saucepan, bring vegetable broth (or water) to a boil. Stir in couscous, cover, and remove from heat. Let it sit for 5 minutes, then fluff with a fork.
- In a large bowl, combine cooked couscous, cherry tomatoes, diced cucumber, sliced Kalamata olives, finely chopped red onion, crumbled feta cheese, and chopped fresh parsley.
- Drizzle olive oil over the salad and season with salt and black pepper. Toss to combine all the ingredients.
- Serve the Grilled Lemon Herb Chicken over a bed of Mediterranean Couscous Salad.

Enjoy this refreshing and wholesome grilled lemon herb chicken with a flavorful Mediterranean couscous salad!

Grilled Vegetable Quesadillas with Avocado Lime Dip

Ingredients:

For the Grilled Vegetables:

- Zucchini, sliced
- Yellow squash, sliced
- Red bell pepper, sliced
- Red onion, sliced
- Cherry tomatoes, halved
- 2 tablespoons olive oil
- 1 teaspoon ground cumin
- 1 teaspoon smoked paprika
- Salt and black pepper to taste

For the Avocado Lime Dip:

- 2 ripe avocados
- Juice of 2 limes
- 1 clove garlic, minced
- 2 tablespoons fresh cilantro, chopped
- Salt and black pepper to taste

For the Quesadillas:

- Flour tortillas
- Shredded cheese (cheddar or Mexican blend)
- Grilled vegetables

- Avocado Lime Dip (from above)

Instructions:

For the Grilled Vegetables:

> In a bowl, toss zucchini, yellow squash, red bell pepper, red onion, and cherry tomatoes with olive oil, ground cumin, smoked paprika, salt, and black pepper.
>
> Grill the vegetables for about 8-10 minutes, turning occasionally, until they are tender and have a nice char.
>
> Remove the grilled vegetables from the grill and set aside.

For the Avocado Lime Dip:

> In a bowl, mash the ripe avocados.
>
> Add lime juice, minced garlic, chopped fresh cilantro, salt, and black pepper. Mix until well combined.
>
> Adjust the seasoning to taste.

For the Quesadillas:

> Preheat the grill or a grill pan to medium-high heat.
>
> Place a tortilla on the grill and sprinkle shredded cheese over one half of the tortilla.
>
> Add a portion of the grilled vegetables on top of the cheese.
>
> Fold the tortilla over to create a half-moon shape.
>
> Grill the quesadilla for about 2-3 minutes per side, or until the cheese is melted and the tortilla is golden.
>
> Repeat the process for additional quesadillas.
>
> Serve the Grilled Vegetable Quesadillas with Avocado Lime Dip on the side.

Enjoy these flavorful and satisfying grilled vegetable quesadillas with a creamy avocado lime dip!

Grilled Shrimp Tacos with Mango Salsa

Ingredients:

For the Grilled Shrimp:

- 1 lb large shrimp, peeled and deveined
- 2 tablespoons olive oil
- 1 teaspoon ground cumin
- 1 teaspoon chili powder
- 1 teaspoon smoked paprika
- Juice of 1 lime
- Salt and black pepper to taste

For the Mango Salsa:

- 1 ripe mango, peeled and diced
- 1/2 red onion, finely chopped
- 1/4 cup fresh cilantro, chopped
- Juice of 1 lime
- Salt to taste

For the Tacos:

- Corn or flour tortillas
- Shredded cabbage or lettuce
- Avocado slices
- Sour cream or Greek yogurt (optional)
- Lime wedges (for serving)

Instructions:

For the Grilled Shrimp:

In a bowl, combine olive oil, ground cumin, chili powder, smoked paprika, lime juice, salt, and black pepper.

Toss the shrimp in the marinade until well-coated. Marinate for at least 15-20 minutes.

Preheat the grill to medium-high heat.

Thread the marinated shrimp onto skewers.

Grill the shrimp skewers for about 2-3 minutes per side, or until the shrimp are opaque and have grill marks.

Remove the grilled shrimp from the skewers and set aside.

For the Mango Salsa:

In a bowl, combine diced mango, finely chopped red onion, chopped fresh cilantro, lime juice, and salt. Mix well.

Adjust the seasoning to taste.

For the Tacos:

Warm the tortillas on the grill for about 10 seconds per side.

Assemble the tacos by placing shredded cabbage or lettuce on each tortilla.

Top with grilled shrimp, mango salsa, avocado slices, and a dollop of sour cream or Greek yogurt if desired.

Serve the Grilled Shrimp Tacos with Mango Salsa hot, accompanied by lime wedges.

Enjoy these vibrant and delicious grilled shrimp tacos with a refreshing mango salsa!

Grilled Chicken Caesar Salad Wraps

Ingredients:

For the Grilled Chicken:

- 1.5 lbs boneless, skinless chicken breasts
- 3 tablespoons olive oil
- 2 cloves garlic, minced
- 1 teaspoon dried oregano
- Salt and black pepper to taste

For the Caesar Dressing:

- 1/2 cup mayonnaise
- 1/4 cup grated Parmesan cheese
- 2 tablespoons Dijon mustard
- 2 tablespoons lemon juice
- 2 cloves garlic, minced
- Salt and black pepper to taste

For the Salad Wraps:

- Romaine lettuce leaves, washed and dried
- Cherry tomatoes, halved
- Croutons
- Shaved Parmesan cheese

Instructions:

For the Grilled Chicken:

In a bowl, whisk together olive oil, minced garlic, dried oregano, salt, and black pepper.

Place the chicken breasts in a shallow dish and pour the marinade over them. Ensure the chicken is well-coated. Marinate for at least 30 minutes.

Preheat the grill to medium-high heat.

Grill the chicken breasts for about 6-7 minutes per side, or until they are cooked through and have grill marks.

Remove the grilled chicken from the grill and let it rest for a few minutes before slicing.

For the Caesar Dressing:

In a bowl, whisk together mayonnaise, grated Parmesan cheese, Dijon mustard, lemon juice, minced garlic, salt, and black pepper. Adjust the seasoning to taste.

For the Salad Wraps:

Lay out individual Romaine lettuce leaves.

Place sliced grilled chicken on each lettuce leaf.

Top with cherry tomatoes, croutons, and shaved Parmesan cheese.

Drizzle Caesar dressing over each wrap.

Fold the sides of the lettuce leaves and roll them up to create the wraps.

Serve the Grilled Chicken Caesar Salad Wraps immediately, offering a light and flavorful meal.

Enjoy these delicious and convenient grilled chicken Caesar salad wraps for a satisfying and refreshing lunch or dinner!

Grilled Vegetable and Pesto Pizza

Ingredients:

For the Pesto Sauce:

- 2 cups fresh basil leaves
- 1/2 cup grated Parmesan cheese
- 1/2 cup pine nuts
- 3 cloves garlic
- 1/2 cup extra-virgin olive oil
- Salt and black pepper to taste

For the Grilled Vegetables:

- Zucchini, thinly sliced
- Yellow squash, thinly sliced
- Red bell pepper, thinly sliced
- Red onion, thinly sliced
- Cherry tomatoes, halved
- 2 tablespoons olive oil
- Salt and black pepper to taste

For the Pizza:

- Pizza dough (store-bought or homemade)
- Shredded mozzarella cheese
- Grated Parmesan cheese
- Fresh basil leaves (for garnish)

Instructions:

For the Pesto Sauce:

In a food processor, combine fresh basil leaves, grated Parmesan cheese, pine nuts, and garlic.

Pulse until the ingredients are finely chopped.

With the food processor running, slowly drizzle in the olive oil until the pesto reaches a smooth consistency.

Season with salt and black pepper to taste. Set aside.

For the Grilled Vegetables:

Preheat the grill to medium-high heat.

In a bowl, toss zucchini, yellow squash, red bell pepper, red onion, and cherry tomatoes with olive oil, salt, and black pepper.

Grill the vegetables for about 5-7 minutes, turning occasionally, until they are tender and have grill marks. Remove from the grill and set aside.

For the Pizza:

Preheat the grill to medium-high heat.

Roll out the pizza dough into your desired shape and thickness.

Carefully transfer the rolled-out pizza dough to the preheated grill.

Grill the pizza dough for about 2-3 minutes per side, or until it has grill marks and is cooked through.

Remove the grilled pizza dough from the grill.

Spread a layer of pesto sauce over the grilled pizza dough.

Arrange the grilled vegetables over the pesto sauce.

Sprinkle with shredded mozzarella cheese and grated Parmesan cheese.

Return the pizza to the grill and close the lid. Grill for an additional 5-7 minutes, or until the cheese is melted and bubbly.

Remove the grilled vegetable and pesto pizza from the grill.

Garnish with fresh basil leaves.

Slice and serve hot.

Enjoy this delicious and vibrant grilled vegetable and pesto pizza for a flavorful and satisfying meal!

Grilled Teriyaki Salmon with Pineapple Salsa

Ingredients:

For the Teriyaki Marinade:

- 4 salmon fillets
- 1/2 cup soy sauce
- 1/4 cup pineapple juice
- 2 tablespoons honey
- 1 tablespoon rice vinegar
- 1 teaspoon sesame oil
- 2 cloves garlic, minced
- 1 teaspoon ginger, grated
- Sesame seeds (for garnish)

For the Pineapple Salsa:

- 1 cup fresh pineapple, diced
- 1/2 red bell pepper, finely chopped
- 1/4 red onion, finely chopped
- 1/4 cup fresh cilantro, chopped
- Juice of 1 lime
- Salt and black pepper to taste

Instructions:

For the Teriyaki Salmon:

In a bowl, whisk together soy sauce, pineapple juice, honey, rice vinegar, sesame oil, minced garlic, and grated ginger to create the teriyaki marinade.

Place the salmon fillets in a shallow dish and pour the marinade over them. Ensure the salmon is well-coated. Marinate for at least 30 minutes.

Preheat the grill to medium-high heat.

Grill the salmon fillets for about 4-5 minutes per side, or until they are cooked through and have grill marks.

During grilling, baste the salmon with any remaining teriyaki marinade for extra flavor. Once the salmon is done, transfer it to a serving platter.

Garnish with sesame seeds.

For the Pineapple Salsa:

In a bowl, combine diced fresh pineapple, finely chopped red bell pepper, finely chopped red onion, chopped fresh cilantro, lime juice, salt, and black pepper. Mix well.

Adjust the seasoning to taste.

To Serve:

Spoon the pineapple salsa over the grilled teriyaki salmon fillets.

Serve the Grilled Teriyaki Salmon with Pineapple Salsa hot.

Enjoy this delightful combination of grilled teriyaki salmon and fresh pineapple salsa for a burst of tropical flavors!

Grilled Vegetable and Quinoa Stuffed Acorn Squash

Ingredients:

For the Quinoa:

- 1 cup quinoa, rinsed
- 2 cups vegetable broth or water
- 1 teaspoon olive oil
- Salt to taste

For the Grilled Vegetables:

- Zucchini, diced
- Red bell pepper, diced
- Red onion, diced
- Cherry tomatoes, halved
- 2 tablespoons olive oil
- 1 teaspoon dried Italian herbs
- Salt and black pepper to taste

For the Stuffed Acorn Squash:

- 2 acorn squash, halved and seeds removed
- Olive oil for brushing
- Salt and black pepper to taste

For Assembly:

- Crumbled feta cheese or goat cheese

- Fresh parsley, chopped
- Balsamic glaze (optional)

Instructions:

For the Quinoa:

Rinse quinoa under cold water. In a saucepan, combine quinoa, vegetable broth (or water), olive oil, and a pinch of salt. Bring to a boil, then reduce heat, cover, and simmer until quinoa is cooked and liquid is absorbed. Fluff with a fork and set aside.

For the Grilled Vegetables:

Preheat the grill to medium-high heat.
In a bowl, toss diced zucchini, diced red bell pepper, diced red onion, and halved cherry tomatoes with olive oil, dried Italian herbs, salt, and black pepper.
Grill the vegetables for about 8-10 minutes, turning occasionally, until they are tender and have a nice char.
Remove the grilled vegetables from the grill and set aside.

For the Stuffed Acorn Squash:

Preheat the grill to medium-high heat.
Brush the cut sides of the acorn squash with olive oil and season with salt and black pepper.
Grill the acorn squash, cut side down, for about 10-12 minutes, or until they are tender and have grill marks.
Once the acorn squash is done, fill each half with a portion of cooked quinoa and grilled vegetables.

Top with crumbled feta cheese or goat cheese.

Garnish with fresh chopped parsley and drizzle with balsamic glaze if desired.

Serve the Grilled Vegetable and Quinoa Stuffed Acorn Squash hot.

Enjoy this wholesome and flavorful grilled vegetable and quinoa stuffed acorn squash as a satisfying and nutritious meal!

Grilled Honey Mustard Chicken Skewers

Ingredients:

For the Honey Mustard Marinade:

- 1/4 cup Dijon mustard
- 3 tablespoons honey
- 2 tablespoons soy sauce
- 2 cloves garlic, minced
- 1 tablespoon olive oil
- 1 teaspoon dried thyme
- Salt and black pepper to taste

For the Chicken Skewers:

- 1.5 lbs boneless, skinless chicken breasts, cut into cubes
- Bell peppers, cut into chunks
- Red onion, cut into chunks
- Cherry tomatoes
- Wooden skewers, soaked in water for 30 minutes

Instructions:

For the Honey Mustard Marinade:

In a bowl, whisk together Dijon mustard, honey, soy sauce, minced garlic, olive oil, dried thyme, salt, and black pepper.

Set aside a portion of the marinade for basting during grilling.

For the Chicken Skewers:

Place the chicken cubes in a shallow dish and pour the honey mustard marinade over them. Ensure the chicken is well-coated. Marinate for at least 30 minutes.

Preheat the grill to medium-high heat.

Thread marinated chicken cubes, bell pepper chunks, red onion chunks, and cherry tomatoes onto soaked wooden skewers, alternating for a colorful mix.

Grill the skewers for about 8-10 minutes, turning occasionally, until the chicken is cooked through and has grill marks.

During grilling, baste the skewers with the reserved honey mustard marinade for extra flavor.

Once the skewers are done, transfer them to a serving platter.

Serve the Grilled Honey Mustard Chicken Skewers hot, accompanied by your favorite side dishes.

Enjoy these sweet and tangy grilled honey mustard chicken skewers for a delightful and easy-to-make meal!

Grilled Halloumi and Vegetable Kabobs

Ingredients:

For the Marinade:

- 1/4 cup olive oil
- 2 tablespoons lemon juice
- 2 cloves garlic, minced
- 1 teaspoon dried oregano
- 1 teaspoon smoked paprika
- Salt and black pepper to taste

For the Kabobs:

- Halloumi cheese, cut into cubes
- Cherry tomatoes
- Zucchini, sliced
- Red bell pepper, cut into chunks
- Red onion, cut into chunks
- Wooden skewers, soaked in water for 30 minutes

Instructions:

For the Marinade:

In a bowl, whisk together olive oil, lemon juice, minced garlic, dried oregano, smoked paprika, salt, and black pepper to create the marinade.
Set aside a portion of the marinade for basting during grilling.

For the Kabobs:

Cut halloumi cheese into cubes.

In a shallow dish, combine halloumi cubes, cherry tomatoes, sliced zucchini, red bell pepper chunks, and red onion chunks.

Pour the marinade over the ingredients and toss gently to coat. Marinate for at least 30 minutes.

Preheat the grill to medium-high heat.

Thread marinated halloumi, cherry tomatoes, zucchini slices, red bell pepper, and red onion onto soaked wooden skewers, alternating for a colorful mix.

Grill the kabobs for about 5-7 minutes, turning occasionally, until the halloumi is golden and has grill marks.

During grilling, baste the kabobs with the reserved marinade for extra flavor.

Once the kabobs are done, transfer them to a serving platter.

Serve the Grilled Halloumi and Vegetable Kabobs hot, offering a delightful and flavorful vegetarian dish.

Enjoy these tasty and satisfying grilled halloumi and vegetable kabobs as a perfect addition to your summer grilling menu!

Grilled Portobello Mushroom Steaks with Chimichurri Sauce

Ingredients:

For the Portobello Mushroom Steaks:

- 4 large portobello mushroom caps, stems removed
- 3 tablespoons balsamic vinegar
- 2 tablespoons soy sauce
- 2 tablespoons olive oil
- 2 cloves garlic, minced
- 1 teaspoon dried thyme
- Salt and black pepper to taste

For the Chimichurri Sauce:

- 1 cup fresh parsley, chopped
- 1/4 cup fresh cilantro, chopped
- 3 cloves garlic, minced
- 1/2 cup extra-virgin olive oil
- 2 tablespoons red wine vinegar
- 1 teaspoon dried oregano
- 1/2 teaspoon red pepper flakes (optional)
- Salt and black pepper to taste

Instructions:

For the Portobello Mushroom Steaks:

In a bowl, whisk together balsamic vinegar, soy sauce, olive oil, minced garlic, dried thyme, salt, and black pepper.

Brush both sides of the portobello mushroom caps with the marinade, ensuring they are well-coated. Marinate for at least 30 minutes.

Preheat the grill to medium-high heat.

Grill the marinated portobello mushroom caps for about 4-5 minutes per side, or until they are tender and have grill marks.

While grilling, baste the mushroom caps with any remaining marinade for extra flavor.

Once the portobello mushroom steaks are done, transfer them to a serving platter.

For the Chimichurri Sauce:

In a bowl, combine chopped fresh parsley, chopped fresh cilantro, minced garlic, extra-virgin olive oil, red wine vinegar, dried oregano, red pepper flakes (if using), salt, and black pepper. Mix well.

Adjust the seasoning to taste.

To Serve:

Drizzle the chimichurri sauce over the grilled portobello mushroom steaks.

Serve the Grilled Portobello Mushroom Steaks with Chimichurri Sauce hot, offering a flavorful and satisfying vegetarian dish.

Enjoy these delicious and hearty grilled portobello mushroom steaks with the zesty kick of chimichurri sauce!

Grilled Vegetable and Goat Cheese Stuffed Bell Peppers

Ingredients:

For the Grilled Vegetables:

- Zucchini, sliced
- Yellow squash, sliced
- Red bell pepper, sliced
- Red onion, sliced
- Cherry tomatoes, halved
- 2 tablespoons olive oil
- 1 teaspoon dried Italian herbs
- Salt and black pepper to taste

For the Stuffed Bell Peppers:

- 4 large bell peppers (assorted colors), halved and seeds removed
- Grilled vegetables (from above)
- 4 oz goat cheese, crumbled
- Fresh basil leaves, chopped
- Balsamic glaze (optional, for drizzling)

Instructions:

For the Grilled Vegetables:

Preheat the grill to medium-high heat.

In a bowl, toss zucchini, yellow squash, red bell pepper, red onion, and cherry tomatoes with olive oil, dried Italian herbs, salt, and black pepper.

Grill the vegetables for about 8-10 minutes, turning occasionally, until they are tender and have a nice char.

Remove the grilled vegetables from the grill and set aside.

For the Stuffed Bell Peppers:

Preheat the grill to medium-high heat.

Clean bell peppers, halve them, and remove the seeds.

Fill each bell pepper half with a generous portion of the grilled vegetables.

Top the vegetables with crumbled goat cheese.

Place the stuffed bell peppers on the grill for an additional 5-7 minutes, or until they are heated through and the goat cheese is slightly melted.

Once the stuffed bell peppers are done, transfer them to a serving platter.

Sprinkle chopped fresh basil over the stuffed peppers.

Drizzle with balsamic glaze if desired.

Serve the Grilled Vegetable and Goat Cheese Stuffed Bell Peppers hot.

Enjoy these flavorful and colorful grilled vegetable and goat cheese stuffed bell peppers as a delightful and nutritious meal!